atara
press

Gad Granach

Where Is Home?

GAD GRANACH

Where Is Home?

Stories from the Life of a German-Jewish Émigré

Translated from the German by David Edward Lane

Atara Press

Based on conversations with Gad Granach conducted by
Hilde Recher, Henryk Broder, and Michael Bergmann.
Hebrew and Yiddish terms appear in the glossary.

First edition: March 2009
Published by Atara Press, Los Angeles
Library of Congress Control Number: 2008941583
English translation copyright © 2007 David Edward Lane
Photos: Private archive of Gad Granach, Jerusalem
Originally published as *Heimat los! Aus dem Leben eines
jüdischen Emigranten* by Oelbaum Verlag, Ausburg
Printed in the United States of America
ISBN-13: 978-0-9822251-1-0

*I don't know why everyone has to go searching
for their identity. For me, they told me my name
and that was all I needed.*

CHAPTER ONE

I was present at my birth but I don't remember it. It was on the 29th of March, 1915, in Rheinsberg, a town as Prussian as could be. My mother was such a great admirer of the dramatist August Strindberg that I was nearly named August after him. Aunt Rosel, however, her youngest sister, saved me from that. Mother had moved from Berlin to Rheinsberg the year before, and found lodging with the refined and noble von Brandes family. Frau von Brandes had hopes she might name me Fritz, after their son who died fighting in the war. Anyhow, Aunt Rosel took one look in the crib, and at the sight of the little Jewish baby boy with a big nose said, "Oh for Heaven's sake, him... an August?" So together they came up with the nice German name Gerhard. What can you do? All German-Jewish boys back then had names like Gerhard, Peter, or Siegfried. If somebody was a Siegfried, you could be certain he was a Jew. I would have preferred the name Peter, however. *Peterchen* I liked as it always went over well with ladies.

My father was absent at my birth, due to the war, of course. He could never feel too comfortable around my mother's family, who were all opposed to the relationship. My father was an *ostjude*, an Eastern European Jew from Galicia, and an artist on top of that. This, for my grandfather, who considered himself a German Jew through and through, was not at all appropriate. He condescendingly referred to my father as the "Galizianer."[1] Petite bourgeoisie are the same all around the world, regardless whether they're Jews or Gentiles.

My mother, Martha Guttmann, belonged to the younger culture-hungry crowd and moved in Berlin's anarcho-syndicalist[2] circles. One was oh-so-modern and progressive then, into nudist culture, homeopathy, and vegetarianism. One revered Strindberg, Ibsen[3], and the modern painters. Everything was all mixed up. There were the anarchists, the syndicalists, and hundreds of saviors with long hair who claimed they had been sent by God to save the world running around.

It was in that world that my mother met my father and immediately fell passionately in love with him, in this elemental force, in this seething something. He had just come from Eastern Europe and was studying at the renowned Max Rheinhardt Acting School, paying his way through by polishing coffins. She was twenty-nine then, and he was four years younger. He still had the famous bowed legs which he wrote about in his memoirs, *There Goes an Actor*, later having them straightened in an operation. My mother helped my father become familiar not only with German culture but with culture in general. She didn't just read Strindberg with him, she gave him his first toothbrush. People gladly forget these sorts of things later, as my father quickly did. In Berlin back then, people frequented the café *Groessenwahn* on Kurfürstendamm,[4] later renamed *Café des Westens*, and which today is *Kran-*

Martha Guttmann and Alexander Granach, Graz 1914

zler. Writers and revolutionaries, left-wingers and right-wingers all gathered there. In those days, my father was even close friends with the poet and dramatist Arnolt Bronnen[5] who later sympathized with the Nazis.

I was conceived shortly before my father was drafted into the war in 1914. As an Austrian citizen, he had to return and join a garrison in Graz. He wrote to my mother: "Martha, I'm going into the field with a solid feeling that nothing will happen to me. There's one thing that's certain: As long as I exist, the world exists! Without me, the world is no longer. Yours, Alex." Father was an enormous optimist. After the war, however, he forgot to come home. He went on to Munich and did theater under the direction of Hermine Koerner.[6]

When I was one year old my mother moved with me back to Berlin, to a place on Regensburger Strasse. There I grew up with several aunts and a grandfather, overly doted on, pampered, and spoiled. The effect of all this somehow still shows in me today. Aunt Rosel worked as a buyer in the leather goods department of KaDeWe.[7] As Fraeulein Guttmann, she was well known in Berlin. To be a sales manager at KaDeWe back then was a big deal. Occasionally I went to visit her in the afternoon at the department store. She would look me up and down with disapproval and say, "Oh no...look at you!" Then I'd find myself being whisked up to the young boys department and would hear, "My nephew. Outfit him, please." Aunt Rosel is a story unto herself. The household was run by Aunt Hedel and Grandfather and nobody was allowed in the kitchen but him. He cursed while he cooked. I think I inherited my

Gad Granach with his mother, Berlin 1917

passion for cooking from him, as well as all the cursing.

My mother's family came from Posen. It was Kurt Tucholsky[8] who said that all Berlin Jews came from either Breslau or Posen.[9] The Jews from Posen felt very German as they had been occupied before and wanted to show their loyalty. For this reason, a prevailing majority in 1919 opted for German and not Polish citizenship. When Posen ultimately became Polish, they were then expelled. My grandfather's brother had a hotel in Kobylin that he did not want to leave behind. He opted for Poland and was allowed to stay. This cost him his life. At the age of 85, the Nazis deported him and his wife to Theresienstadt.

My grandfather's name was Abraham Adolf Guttmann,

and he had been an Imperial soldier in the Prussian army. He served 1870-71 in Glogau. When Kaiser Wilhelm II had to abdicate in 1918, he wept. It seemed like he took it more to heart than the Kaiser himself did. His old uniform hung in the attic, and I used to play with it, putting the cap on my head and marching out in the street.

My mother was an official at the city employment office in Berlin. She became a member of the USPD[10] party but was later bitterly disappointed by them. She would never have joined the SPD[11] though. For them she was too much of an intellectual. Those at the employment office certainly didn't like this fact as the place was full of SPD bigwigs. Later they were as prepared as all the others to cooperate with anyone and everyone, including the devil. They even would have made a pact with Hitler if he had allowed it. Anything for the sake of dear peace.

Father said to me once when I was just fourteen, "Your mother is so petit bourgeois!" I was shaken, understanding this as some kind of insult. In my eyes, she was an open-minded, progressive, educated woman, immensely interested in everything going on in the world. I have her to thank for my first lesson in politics—as a young boy she gave me Kropotkin's "Mutual Aid." My first Traven[12] series books were also from her.[13] She strove to open my eyes to my surroundings. I was not allowed to read any of the Indian books popular with German boys then, only Fenimore Cooper's "The Leatherstocking Tales." Karl May[14] was strictly *verboten*. Of course, I didn't have any toy soldiers either, though naturally I would have loved some. Mother had a good, respectable position at the city employment office and was in every sense the opposite of my father. Basically, she really was petit bourgeois.

I did not meet my father until I was four years old. He came back to Berlin in 1919, still wearing his military uniform. With his cap and bayonet by his side, he made a huge impression on me. My mother simply said, "This is your father." I then spoke the legendary sentence that my family would relish retelling again and again: "Wat denn, wat denn, det soll mein Vater sein?" (Wait, wait...is he really supposed to be my father?) They all thought this was marvelous; so sophisticated for a four-year-old. A *wunderkind*! My father then lifted me up kissed me. He was unshaven and his beard scratched me. That was my first encounter with him. In 1921 they divorced. Actually, it was my mother who divorced him.

Although my parents never really did live together, I still had a hard time understanding why they separated. We never had a family life together in the typical sense. My parents were not a good match for each other. They did have a wild time together before the war, but that was all. My mother simply was not cut out for his lifestyle. She was a woman from a respectable middle-class family engaged in political issues. Father, in contrast, was an artist moving up in his career, and she was holding him back. Politics and bohemia do not fit together well. As long as he was naïve and a nobody, still learning German and dependent on her for his education and culture, everything was fine. But when he began to stand on his own two feet, becoming

Gad Granach with his father, Berlin 1919

more independent and moving in larger circles, he went on to places where my mother could not go and did not want to go. She was a bit like a mother hen raising a duckling. One day the duckling goes to the water and swims away. The hen then stands at the water's edge and no longer understands the world anymore. My mother too was at a loss to fully comprehend what had happened. Up to her final days she still did not really understand. She adored and idolized my father, yet she hated him at the same time. When he became famous, the Berlin papers were filled with his escapades, scandals, and affairs. She couldn't handle this. She never remarried and from then on had only platonic friendships with men.

Mother liked to surround herself with enthusiastic young poets and philosophers. I remember one in particular who I absolutely could not stand. Children can be terribly snobby in their own way. This man, a brother of the famous violinist Bronislaw Hubermann,[15] was one of those starving philosophers, a depraved genius, and absolutely inept at living. He came over for supper every Thursday evening. It was probably Hubermann's only meal the entire week. My mother would have done better to serve something solid and hearty, but they were all living oh-so healthy then. Normally, there were two hard-boiled eggs, some herring, bread and butter, slices of cheese, and beer. When Hubermann came, there was just beer. A group of like-minded single women who wore wool underclothes were invited over, and they all sat around him engrossed. *Blaustruempfe* "blue stockings" they used to call them. I used to imagine that they actually wore blue stockings. They were all rather distinguished, enormously intellectual, and 100% asexual. The clothes they wore were *gesundheitskleidern*, "health clothing" from "Indanthren."

So Hubermann would come over, read from his own writings, and my mother would always go, "Shhh!" It was very boring for me, namely because I couldn't make any noise. She constantly surrounded herself with the ineffectual starving artist/writer types who came to us and read from their works. There is a sad footnote to Hubermann's story. In the 1930's, he was found dead in his room. He died of starvation. His famous brother, a virtuoso on the violin but not much of a human being, had sent him 200 Marks which Hubermann promptly sent back. At some point he stopped coming over, and my mother expressed grave concern that she hadn't done enough to help him.

Around this time I was given a violin. Back then, a young boy violinist named Yehudi Menuhin[16] was heralded as a *wunderkind*, and all Jewish parents were convinced that they too might have a virtuoso at home. So I was forced— and I do emphasize the word "forced"—to take violin lessons. I stood at the window struggling to play *Alle meine Entchen* (All My Little Ducklings) on the instrument, while down below in the street I could see children playing. I preferred pretending the violin case was a boat and playing with it on the carpet. I had the feeling right from the very start that these violin lessons were a waste of time. After one year, thankfully, my violin instructor realized this too. I wasn't the only victim of Yehudi Menuhin, though. There were hundreds of Jewish boys who suddenly had a chunk of wood stuck under their chin, a bow placed in their hand, and no clue as to why this was happening to them. They practiced screeching and squeaking on the instrument to the horror of neighbors, dogs and cats alike.

My mother went along with every modern passing fad. She wore *reformkleider*, clothing to promote wellness, and shopped at health food stores. Berlin in those days was filled with charlatans and crooks. The first to appear was Lukutate. This trickster wore a turban and sold an unspeakably strange tasting marmalade. In many a pharmacy window was an Indian with a turban and a spear atop a huge elephant, while underneath it read, "The Power of

Vacation in Fuessen

an Elephant is the Power of Lukutate!!!" His concoctions were supposedly made from green plant extracts collected in India, combined alphabetically or something, and made into a purée. I'm sure it was really just cabbage heads from Berlin. My mother bought it all: Lukutate jam, Lukutate pastries, Lukutate lozenges, Lukutate cream, and Lukutate powder. We used it all over our bodies, inside and out. I believed I'd soon start to grow elephant tusks. Lukutate was fantastic, but humanity did not become any wiser from it.

My mother was also a member of a vegetarian sect in Berlin called "Masdasnan." Masdasnan came from America and persuaded people to believe they should not ingest anything whatsoever from animals. No animal products for clothing either; no leather shoes, no wool, just linen. I wouldn't be surprised if this particular oddity came from Judaism as Jews are also not supposed to mix wool and linen together. Why this is, I do not know, and if I did, I'd be a head rabbi somewhere in Israel or America by now. In any event, Masdasnan followers had to wrap themselves up in white robes and could only eat raw vegetables that grew above ground. I think in the end, you were supposed to stop eating all together. There was a restaurant on Fehrbelliner Platz with items like meatless fake sausages, probably made from old bar stool legs, or some other mysterious ingredients.

My mother actually believed in this Masdasnan nonsense until the day she had a breakdown. Then the doctor advised her, "Dear Frau, I want you to go down around the corner this instant to the first butcher you find and buy two large steaks, one for you and one for your son. Do this every day for a week and then come back to see me." At home, however, we had a nanny who acted like the Gestapo for Masdasnan, and we were afraid of her. She was completely insane. She had hair parted straight down the middle with rolled buns on either side and always went around shouting "Hallelujah!" She was fired after the third steak.

It was a turbulent time in Berlin. One of my earliest memories is of the Rathenau[17] murder. I believed I had glimpsed his killers when I was around six. Like most children in post-WWI Germany, I was a bit undernourished. To freshen me up, my parents sent me to Lunenburg Heath in the countryside for the summer break. A family I lived with there, the Bornemanns, had an apple farm and a horse. One day I was playing in the street with the other kids when suddenly a couple of policeman on motorcycles came speeding down the road. They hit the brakes by us and asked if we had just seen two men on bicycles. "Sure, we saw 'em" we promptly replied, our imaginations getting the better of us. I'm still convinced to this day I saw them and that they were Rathenau's murderers.

I didn't attend a Jewish school even though my mother came from an observant family. We were proud of being Jewish, and at the same time, we felt very German as well. German and Jewish went together marvelously! My grandfather was a real German nationalist, yet he was also a loyal and faithful Jew. He was a synagogue caretaker, a *shammes,* and went to the one on Luetzow-Ufer to open and close it everyday. He died in 1921. His grave is located in Berlin-Weissensee. There he rests, together with his wife who was run over by a beer wagon in 1905. She always daydreamed while she walked.

In 1921, after grandfather's death, we moved to Friedenau. It was already becoming a real Nazi area, however. When I was six, I entered primary school, but my mother had to pull me out two years later because our teacher was a Nazi. Even in 1923, he was coming to the school with a swastika pin on his coat.

Berlin, 1923

One day as I was playing in the street, a young boy around my age approached me and said, "Me and my parents, we're anti-Semites." He was wearing a cap with the word *Vaterland* on it and was dressed in a little sailor suit, the kind with a cinched belt and tight in the ass. I knew him from across the street. He actually came right out and said, "Me and my parents are anti-Semites." I had no idea what he was talking about. He could just as well have said, "Me and my parents, we're from Mongolia." I don't know why, but I never did tell my mother anything about it.

We were the only Jews on our street. Around us were nothing but nationalistic-minded petit bourgeois types, either Nazis or people who were mentally still living in pre-WWI Imperial times, the days of the German Kaiserreich. As in the Kaiser's time, they celebrated the Kaiser's birthday and hung black, white, and red flags out of their windows. The black, red, and gold flag of the Weimar Republic was nowhere to be seen as this was the flag of the "Judenrepublik," or "Jewish Republic"; that's what the right-wing groups called the Weimar Republic. In contrast, what hung on the walls in our home were the pictures that all upstanding Western Jewish families had: Heine, Goethe, Napoleon who had emancipated the Jews, and also Michaelangelo's Moses of course. As a kid, I saw Moses as a fellow countryman who led the Jews through the Red Sea and did all kinds of fantastic stuff on Mount Sinai.

I was not raised religiously at all, yet I simply had a feeling of to whom I belonged. I was told that Jews should defend themselves and strike back: If somebody at school picks on you for being Jewish, then hit back, don't just sit there and take it. I thought of myself as being very German, too, but at the same time quite proud to be a member of an ancient people. I knew who Albert Einstein was and what we Jews had brought to the German culture. There were plenty of famous authors, doctors, and inventors you could look up to, like the pilot and inventor Otto Lilienthal[18] who, by the way, I'm not so absolutely sure was even Jewish. No matter. Whoever wasn't Jewish could be made Jewish. After all, even Jesus was a Jew, since someone born in Bethlehem certainly was no Aryan. I had tried explaining to my classmates how, ultimately, they had us to thank for all of Christendom and they should be grateful. They didn't get it though, and didn't want to be thankful. A classmate once said to me, "Your people crucified our Jesus." So I asked him, "Were you there?" "Nope," he replied. "Me neither," I said.

After second grade in the Friedenau public school, Mother removed me and enrolled me in a modern school, the Waldschule in Dahlem-Dorf. At the time there was a trend for so-called "Freie Schulen" (literally "free schools," of alternative or progressive nature). This particular school was founded by the Benario Family, very wealthy Berlin Jews who did not want to see their own children attending one of those dreadful post-Wilhelmian schools. The Prussian schools were nothing but a mixture between jail and hospital; germ cells for National Socialism.

The Waldschule Dahlem in contrast was progressive. The pupils there were the children of intellectuals and émigrés, from Czarists to Trotskyites to escaped Leninists, all were represented. Trudchen Nottmann, a very good friend of mine who also lives in Jerusalem, went to that school as well. In my class was the daughter of von Steinberg, a Russian exile whom the then-Minister of Justice, Kerensky,[19] refused to sign a death sentence for. He was, by the way, a devout Jew. These were the kinds of people who sent their kids to such schools, and as my parents always strove to do whatever was modern, I too was sent there. There was, however, one rotten teacher there. She later became the governess of Goering's daughter, but even back then she made spiteful anti-Semitic remarks. She once boxed my

At the Waldschule Dahlem
Gad Granach 2nd row from the bottom, 4th from the right

At the Berlin zoo, 1923

ears in the school's basement, just out of the blue. Nothing like that would ever happen to me again though.

I was definitely happy at the Waldschule. It was a time free from pressure and stress. They didn't use reading primers and textbooks but instead read Moerike and Dr. Uhlebuhle.[20] The children weren't required to stand when a teacher entered, and we could speak to them using the informal case in German.[21] It was wonderful. We didn't have homework and could choose which subjects to study. I picked the one where you don't study at all. Outside there was a vegetable garden and a playground where we built ourselves a huge ship and played *Battleship Potemkin*.[22] I believe those four years were the best ones of my life.

I attended the Waldschule Dahlem up to the age of twelve, and then at home they discovered that I could read, but couldn't write. Actually, I still can't do that properly today. So then I was sent to a another school, to Lehmann's Boys School, on a so-called "Press" or remedial fast-track where teachers helped the students catch up on their grammar and dates in a very old fashioned manner, and where I too was going to make up for my prior neglect. Here the lesson material was really hammered into the students in preparararation for the *Abitur*.[23] But I wasn't a great student there either. By the time I was sixteen, I found I'd had enough, and my parents had as well. Father was always dissatisfied with my performance and mother always just shook her head.

I used to visit my father once a week. On Sundays I was dressed in my best clothes and admonished not to get dirty, "Because that will reflect badly on me," my mother would say, "...and don't horse around on your way over there." So I'd begin my march. The correct route was to take a streetcar to Zoo station and then ride one more station on the subway. To save myself money though, I would go on foot instead, cutting through the Zoological Gardens and watching the animals for a while.

Afterwards, I went to my father's place on Cuxhavener Strasse. He had a fantastic loft there, and it was like another world for me. Mother earned a decent sum as a city employee, and she was a wonderful mother, but making sudden huge leaps up was not part of her plan. With my father it was exactly the opposite. He had become a very popular actor in the meantime and was living in high style. There was always something exciting going on at his place. The apartment would be full of people: actors, writers, philosophers. Among those who visited were Brecht, Piscator, Heinrich Mann, Klabund, Hesse, Heinrich George, Erich Muehsam, and many others.[24] They cooked, ate, drank, and celebrated, and it was all incredibly exciting for me. When I was a little older I could stay the night. Often there were 20 or 30 people there, and then all at once they'd call for taxis. Taxis were still a partly open-air affair then, and at night they raced by like the devil over the *Avus*.[25] People wanted fast-moving cars even then. Father bought his first automobile in 1929, a Chevrolet Sport convertible. Two could sit in the front while in back was a trunk seat known as the *Schwiegermuttersitz*—the "mother-in-law seat." His ladies sat up front with him and I rode in the back, in that little seat. When it came time to return to mother

I became totally depressed, like sunshine turned to rain. Today when I think of Cinderella, it all fits me so perfectly; having to leave the glittering ball behind and return home to a dull gray life with mother.

Father and I became closer the older I got. Yet at the same time, I felt torn. On the one hand, he had left my mother and I felt solidarity with her. On the other hand, I truly admired him and so feared betraying my mother whenever I was with him. It was difficult for me. We later moved again to a better home in Schmargendorf, and father also moved to Dahlem, only five minutes away from us on my bicycle.

He told me a lot about his past and often said, "Come, let me take you to where I came from." He would bring me to the *Scheunenviertel*, the Jewish ghetto of Berlin. Father was never ashamed of his Eastern Jewish background; quite the contrary. By then, however, he spoke very little Yiddish, and tried instead to speak High German exclusively. He did so out of concern for his theater voice. Yiddish can be dangerous because in its expression and melody it's an extremely strong tongue. Like with a hot spice, a pinch too much and it's so overpowering that you can't get rid of it. Yiddish dominates every language, even Hebrew. Rudolph Schildkraut, to the consternation of Max Rheinhardt, could only play the role of Shylock[26] because he spoke with this Yiddish sing-song accent. My father grew up with Yiddish, but he spoke pure, clear German. The only other man with whom I heard him speak Yiddish outside of the *Scheunenviertel* was his friend

Alexander Granach and his mother, Galicia 1915

Chemio Vinaver,[27] a highly gifted musician. He was the choir director for Rabbi Joachim Prinz[28] at Berlin's Friedenstempel (Temple of Peace) and was married to Mascha Kaleko.[29] Chemio was from a Hasidic family, looked very elegant, and could sing wonderfully. He had been an extra with Fritzi Massary[30] once, and would tell the story of how he had to dance with her in a white tailcoat and she said to him during the dance, "Come closer, silly boy."

In the *Scheunenviertel* we would go to "Appelbaum" on Grenadierstrasse and order gefilte fish with lots of horseradish and have schnapps to drink along with it. There the *challah* would be torn apart as is customary, because *challah* is not to be cut. On Grenadierstrasse people came from all sides calling "Granach! Granach's here!" Everyone knew him and called him the "Koenig der Ostjuden"—King of the Eastern Jews. Father was in his element, and I stood like the successor to the throne. The Jews there were not how the anti-Semites wanted to portray them. I was always told at home, "Just don't draw any attention; it produces anti-Semitism." But that didn't help, because regardless of what you did, one way or another you were still a *scheissjud* (shitty Jew). If one was loud, one was a *saujud* (dirty Jew), and if one was quiet, then one was a quiet *saujud*. Anti-Semitism isn't generated from anything; it's simply there.

The Eastern Jews of the *Scheunenviertel* had something truly positive about them. They were militant and self-assured. They weren't ashamed of their Jewishness, which they couldn't have disguised in any case. When German Jews went to the synagogue, they would try to cover up their prayer books as much as possible with the newspaper. You could watch such scenes on Kurfürstendamm before noon on Shabbat. All at once you'd see a procession of elegantly dressed men and women discreetly carrying an object wrapped in newspaper. That wasn't gefilte fish. It was their prayer book.

In contrast, the Jews on Grenadierstrasse in the *Scheunenviertel* were indeed poor, but self-confident. I hadn't realized there was a Jewish proletariat until then; tailors and shoemakers and the like, offering everything one could want or need done, buying and selling as much as possible. They really worked hard. It's not easy to turn a profit selling old trousers! First you have to convince someone that his trousers are no longer any good so he'll sell them to you. Then you have to convinvce someone else that the trousers are really fine threads, first class, so he'll buy them from you. By the end of the day, your nerves are a mess from all the dealing and haggling. It's like an old joke about selling a can of sardines: Yankel sells the can to Moishe, and Moishe sells it again to Simche. Simche exchanges it again with Yankel, and Yankel sells it once more. One day a non-Jew comes and says, "These sardines, they stink!" Yankel says, "What did you do to them then? God forbid, you didn't open them did you?" "Of course I opened them," replies the non-Jew. Yankel then shouts, "Now you've gone and ruined our business! Those sardines are for buying and selling, not eating!" That's how it was in the *Scheunenviertel*. Still, I would never have wished to live there.

I was friends later in Jerusalem with Chemio Vinaver.

I invited him once for a drive through Jerusalem's *Scheunenviertel*, through *Mea Shearim* where our Orthodox Jews live. It's just as much a ghetto, the difference being that they *choose* to live there. So we drove around it together and while observing it all through my Western Jewish eyes I said, "Look at this, Chemio. Isn't it terrible?" But

With father, Berlin 1925

he only responded, *Asoi derf aussehen a Jid!* ("Ah, this is how a real Jew should look!") That was Chemio for you. He was so sentimental that unlike me, he felt just great in *Mea Shearim*. He wasn't religious, in fact, but he still to went to the synagogue on Friday evenings. There he heard sounds which evoked memories of a long-lost home.

My father was exactly the same way. At his place he kept a menorah on the table that during Christmas was dressed up with fir branches. As they say, I was raised sort of Jewish, but Christmas we could also celebrate. Lotte Lieven, his female companion back then, bought a small Christmas tree that my father threw straight out. Lotte was Swiss and was as miserly as they come, buying the cheapest and ugliest tree. He flung the tree down six floors, right through the middle of the stairwell, and ran right out to buy a new one, a gigantic one. But on Yom Kippur, he went to the synagogue to cry his eyes out.

When I was thirteen, I thought it would be nice to have a Bar Mitzvah, but my father was completely against it. He promised me a bicycle if I would just forget about the idea. That was our deal: bicycle instead of Bar Mitzvah. But half a year later I broke my word. "I want to have my Bar Mitzvah!" I said. He became angry and screamed at me, "You swindler! If you think I am going to go with you to the synagogue, then you are terribly mistaken!" But he couldn't escape the whole thing, and in the end he accompanied me to the synagogue.

It was an Orthodox synagogue of Western Jews who worship in an entirely different manner than Eastern Jews. As the father of the Bar Mitzvah boy, he had to accompany me, unrolling the Torah so a section could be read aloud at a time. Jews from the West did all this very discreetly and in a civilized manner, very differently than Eastern Jews.

There's a story about the German Jews who always prayed very quietly, never raising their voice or causing any disturbance for their dear God. One Yom Kippur, an Orthodox Jew from Poland shows up at the German synagogue. He puts on his prayer shawl and then begins to settle all his accounts with God. He beats his chest, bows and swings while crying out, "Oy vey!" and again, "Oy vey!!!" All of Jewish suffering was resting on his shoulders and he had to cry out the pain of two thousand years of persecution and pogroms. Of course there is definitely something to be upset about there; it doesn't come from nowhere. The German Jews glared at him until finally the *shammes* went up to him and quietly said, "You're not going to achieve anything up there by force."

My father basically did the same thing at my Bar Mitzvah. He went up, kissed the *tallis,* the prayer-shawl, and placed it over his head as one should. Then he began to read aloud from the Torah as if he were Moses himself atop Mount Sinai. The whole synagogue shook. Everyone woke up and sat motionless. Even the *shammes*, who usually just shuffled around, stood transfixed. A new wind swept through the synagogue and the rabbi, Emil Cohn, was beaming. When I came up after him to say my portion, the whole thing went straight downhill. He was the star, not I.

We walked from the synagogue to my father's place where he had ordered breakfast from Kempinski to be delivered. Some of the guests came in their Rolls Royces but parked around the corner because, naturally, one does not drive on Shabbat. Joachim Prinz was there too, something of a star rabbi in Berlin then. There was a wonderful buffet with chicken, pigeon, and salad, and we all sat around the table enjoying the meal. Suddenly, Rabbi Emil Cohn says to my father, "Alex, who did you order breakfast from?" "Kempinski, of course" he replies. It was a Jewish establishment. Dismayed, Cohn says, "But Kempinski is not kosher." From that moment on, no one dared take another bite because they all knew the other was watching. Only Joachim Prinz wasn't bothered. He served himself and then me some pigeon and said, "Let's eat." The other guests just drank vodka from then on, and after half an hour, the entire Bar Mitzvah company was rip-roaring drunk. It was great. They were hugging and kissing each other, singing while the table bowed from the weight of the food, which nobody else was touching. That was my Bar Mitzvah.

My first visit to the theater was with my father when I was quite young. I remember it very clearly. It was *Das tapfere Schneiderlein*, "The Brave Little Tailor." He took me backstage at the end and I recall feeling scared to death when I saw how big the tailor was and the long scissors hanging from his trousers. When I was around ten, he began taking me to the real theater but only when he was performing. The first piece I saw was Schiller's *Fiesco* at the *Volksbuehne*, a wonderful theater where the walls were covered in red mahogany.[31] He exposed me to the classics, one after the other but, unfortunately, I often saw just half of a performance. If only he had played the part of Wallenstein, then I could have watched from beginning to end. But he had the role of Isolani. Isolani was on at the beginning and played up until about the middle, then it was over for him, and for me. Herr Isolani goes home, Herr Granach goes home too, and so did I. In *Fiesco zu Genua* he played the part of Mohr who gets hanged in the middle. There again I had to leave before it was over. The usher always quietly came to get me out of the theater; "Pssst! Your father is waiting!" He certainly realized that I didn't like this but only said, "You saw your old father and that's enough." That's why I always saw half performances.

When I was fifteen or sixteen, I listened in on him rehearsing for a particular role, and that's how I discovered my great love of *Faust*. By then he was with the Berlin Prussian State Theater, preparing for the role of Mephisto in *Faust Part II*. I could recite entire passages by heart and still can to this day.

Much later in Jerusalem, I was always performing and translating it for my astounded Israeli guests. I have a friend here, Shmuel Birger, who was so impressed that he's been practicing a few lines of Faust in German for thirty years now. Since German is well nigh impossible for a native born Israeli to pronounce, he still cannot do it properly today: *"Ein guter Mensch in seinem dunklen Drange, ist sich des rechten Weges wohl bewusst"* ("A good man, even in his darker impulses, is well aware of the right way"). He really messes that one up. Whenever I have guests visiting from Germany, I bring him over and have him do his Faust. Folks are quite impressed, and they ask with astonishment, "Does he really speak German?" "Of course he speaks German!" I say. Then he lays one more on them for good measure with, *"Und sich mit Narren zu beladen, das kommt zuletzt dem Teufel noch zu schaden,"* ("To be weighted down by fools, in the end, even the devil cannot help"). That's Mephisto's last line in part two, where during a performance in the emperor's courtyard it is revealed that Faust needn't have fallen in love with Helena, who, it turns out, was only part of a shadow play he had conjured up himself.

That's how it is with people in love, they don't realize that their love is of their own making. When one person hates another, that's of his own making as well. Exactly how anti-Semitism is fundamentally not a Jewish problem, but rather that of the anti-Semite and his sick soul. It has nothing whatsoever to do with us. Anti-Semitism is there, and even if there were no Jews, then they would have to be invented so that men could somehow live out their aggression. Look what happened in Germany. They didn't want the Jews, but now they have the Turks instead. And if they don't want the Turks, then they'll get the Kurds. Fortunately there is always somebody around to hate.

While father was playing *Faust Part II*, he threw a huge party at home. I knew then almost all the important actors, among them Elisabeth Bergner.[32] I had a huge crush on her, and so did my father. My idol, however, was Ernst Busch, whom I also got to meet through my father.[33] They were all always very nice to me. The fact that my father was famous made certain things easier for me and opened many doors. It frequently went something like this: "Ger-

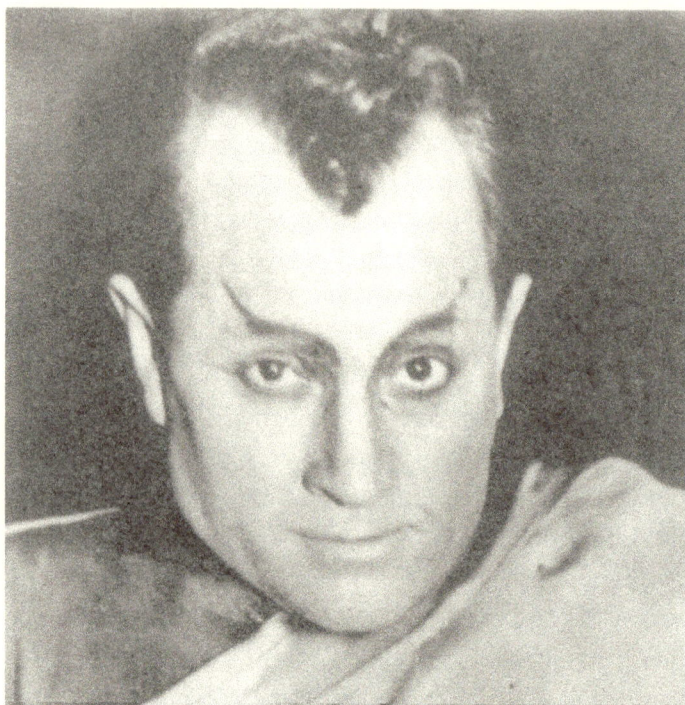

Alexander Granach as Mephisto, Berlin 1933

hard Granach? Are you related to the actor? Oh, you're the son!" Yet I often felt I didn't deserve the attention the name brought.

All of Berlin loved my father. The exception was Max Reinhardt; he did not. Reinhardt, in the meantime, had become the owner of a castle and turned so snooty that he didn't even speak with himself anymore. People forget where they come from most of the time, and Granach reminded Reinhardt of Galicia. My father was a real curiosity to the Berlin taxi drivers because he could drink as much as them. Tossing back schnapps like water was something he learned in Poland, and when he had his leather jacket on they could mistake him for one of their own. He was so proud that the taxi drivers treated him like that because it proved he came across like a real Berliner.

Father was extremely well-read. There was a saying, "Dumb like a tenor" and it applied well to many actors. Their only thoughts were, "Did you see me? How was I?" Father said to me once, "Actors are like empty vessels. What is poured in from above, comes out the bottom." Most couldn't bother themselves with politics, and that was evident as Hitler came to power. Their collaboration was held against them, but then again, why are these actors to blame? They didn't have a clue about anything. Most were completely apolitical. My father was one of the few actors educated in political as well as literary matters. Because he came from the ghetto and had lots of catching up to do, he devoured books. He read everything that came under his nose, not just what my mother recommended. Once when my mother gave him a book by Strindberg, she had to wash it off after he was done. He was working making coffins at the time, and would read while polishing them.

After the First World War, the actress and theater director Hermine Koerner was the most important woman in my father's life. She sponsored him as an actor because she found him to be such a promising talent. He had his breakthrough 1920-21 in Munich and came directly afterwards to Berlin. There he performed in *Der lasterhafte Herr Tschu* ("The Depraved Mr. Tschu") under the direction of

Barnowsky.[34] Father was very big by then and able to demand that Elisabeth Bergner play opposite him as his partner. She was a very close friend of his at the time, a petite, young, fascinating woman, who hadn't yet received any major parts. So it was that Granach brought Ms. Bergner from Vienna to Berlin.

As it turned out, Bergner was a hit in her role but Granach was barely mentioned by the critics. Although everyone knew Elisabeth Bergner used her lovers as a springboard for her career, my father never really got over her. He had many women in his life, but she would remain a taboo subject not to be mentioned. When she devoted an entire chapter to him in her memoirs, I was quite pleased. She wrote how Granach brought her to Berlin and that she had him to thank for her career. She also wrote that he loved only blondes, but that's simply not true. Elisabeth Bergner had indeed been the great love of his life. After my

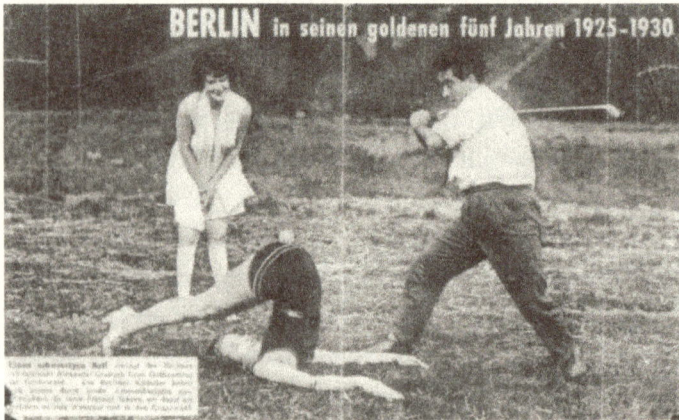

Newspaper story about Alexander Granach

father, came Heinrich George. Over the course of her life, she left many broken hearts behind in her wake. She would simply leave and move on.

My father's appearances at the *Volksbuehne* were a great success, and in between, he acted in some of the very first feature films, including Murnau's 1922 classic *Nosferatu*. He and Murnau knew each other from the Max Reinhardt school. His most significant breakthrough came in 1927, in Ernst Toller's *Hoppla, wir leben!* (Hoppla, Such is Life!) directed by Erwin Piscator. That made him a major star in Berlin. Afterwards, he went to the Berlin Prussian State Theater to Leopold Jessner who was crazy about him.[35] Under Jessner, he could do as he pleased and received the big roles.

Occasionally, my father took me to rehearsals, and as a result, I understood that acting was serious work. People always seem to believe that actors do their performance in the evening and then go out afterwards for a good time, go to bed very late, then fool around the next day until the evening when they can amuse themselves again onstage. But as a kid I saw how disciplined an actor had to be. My father normally awoke at eight in the morning to be at the theater by nine, and remained in rehearsals until midday. Often they would do another run-through in the late afternoon, return home quickly for two hours, then go back to the theatre in the evening. Prussian discipline ruled at the State Theater. They worked hard and earnestly, with no talking back or general hysteria like in the film industry. The director sat down below, and everyone else had very little say in things. Only the stagehands were permitted to keep doing whatever they were up to. They schlepped around and knocked about without any concern, even when a sensitive scene was being rehearsed. Their total disregard astounded me.

There were so-called "matinees" every Sunday in Berlin, usually held by the communists at the Theater on Nollendorfplatz. This was 1930-31 and the Nazi danger was already visible on the horizon. People such as Claire Waldoff, Friedrich Wolf, and Erich Kaestner came and performed, also Muehsam, Tucholsky and of course Ernst Busch.[36] He was the celebrities' celebrity. He sang songs and was the absolute center of attention. Father recited Tucholsky. All the serious artists took part in these matinees, and without charging a fee.

People were very politically engaged then, and father took part in it all. Most of his crowd was left-wing of course, left of the SPD, the Social Democratic Party of Germany. Even Veit Harlan, Renee Stobrawa, and Fritz Genschow were involved, people who later sympathized with the Nazis, having ostensibly been "forced" to do so.[37] Veit Harlan was the first to come driving up with a swastika pennant on his car. Emil Jennings kept himself out of it, but Heinrich George stopped being friends with my father of course. Werner Kraus wasn't in fact a Nazi, but he had always been a raving anti-Semite.[38]

When my father would play Shylock, it was such a demanding performance that he'd be thoroughly exhausted after every evening's performance. An actor could play Shylock in such a way that the audeince could be quite moved, or he could be played the way Werner Kraus did

— 34 —

him, with a new audience leaving the theater every evening as anti-Semites.

Political organizations from the left tried to recruit the big film stars, but it was in vain. Almost all of them were completely apolitical and as such, were easy targets to be manipulated by Goebbels, Hitler's film and propaganda minister.

Naturally, I wanted to become an actor too but my father felt I should at least learn a normal respectable profession first. He convinced me to become a cameraman because that was a job with a new future. So at sixteen I began a photography apprenticeship. That was just about the last thing in the world I wanted to learn. It would have been easy for him to help me succeed in theater, but he wasn't thinking of that. In the next life, however, he can be the cameraman and I'll be the actor.

I went to Karl Trieb's photography studio in Berlin-Steglitz. Trieb was a German nationalist to the core, but also an artist. Here I could observe how National Socialism developed and spread among the petite bourgeoisie, and how Germany slowly collapsed. At first, Karl Trieb was still reading the *Lokalanzeiger* newspaper, but then he changed over to the Nazi party paper, the *Volkischen Beobachter*. His son, also named Gerhard, was in the Hitler Youth and his nephew became an SA officer. During this photographer's apprenticeship, I learned how to polish shoes properly.

Karl Trieb was a very fine portrait photographer, and his clientele were all pure German nationalists but very cultivated people. The entire Brenninkmeyer family came to be photographed by us, famous Catholic anti-Semites, by the way, and proud of it. As the apprentice, I had the task of bringing the clientele up in the elevator. I wore a yellow dustcoat and looked very photogenic, with my hair slicked back with pomade.

Trieb also shot staged scenes in the nude, entirely serious, of course. Back then it was all about strength and beauty as we saw later with Leni Riefenstahl, and *vereine fuer freikoerperkultur*—nudist culture societies, were popping up everywhere. Parents began having their

At Karl Trieb's in Steglitz, Berlin 1932

daughters photographed naked before they were wed. I couldn't believe it! These weren't bohemian types either, but good, upstanding citizens from Steglitz, one of Berlin's wealthiest districts. One time a butcher came, who looked like a butcher should, with his wife who looked like a wild boar, and their very sweet daughter who looked like a little nymphet. I wasn't allowed to be there while she was photographed; the father and mother were there. Their young daughter lay on a Biedermeier chaise lounge with nothing but a thin veil over her and her bosom completely exposed. I saw the photos later, of course.

We also photographed *Burschenschaftler*[39], student dueling societies. They came in full regalia with swords, snappily dressed and very stiff. Their preferred group portrait: two of them resting on the floor, the next row sitting down, and the rest standing in a row behind with a flag on either side. Today I know those were future state attorneys and Nazi judges, with their dueling marks across the face. At Trieb's I heard for the first time that classic sentence, "If all the Jews are like you, then you don't have anything to worry about."

Fortunately, I did worry, and so did my father and mother. The Nazis were running around without restraint, and because I looked very Jewish, I tried to stay out of their path as much as possible. It once happened that I stepped onto the subway, the doors shut, and the entire car was filled with SA; so I squeezed myself into a corner.

One day I picked up my mother at the employment office as we were going out together afterwards to buy some new

Berlin, Friedrichstrasse Station circa 1930

things for me. I was just at that age where everything starts to really grow with boys: the nose gets larger, the ears, and most of all the feet. I entered the room and went over to my mother who was still helping an unemployed woman. "Your son?" she asked. "Ja," my mother said. Again the woman, "You're married to a Jew aren't you?" Mother: "Ja." The woman didn't stop: "So what's the father doing?" Mother wanted to spare herself the explanation of being a divorcée from an actor. "He died in the war, fighting on the front." The woman held her head and exclaimed, "Oh dear God, a Jew and a war widow of a Jew to boot!"—as if one misfortune wasn't enough. Every evening, mother came home from the employment office all shook up over what she had to put up with. One time a woman said to her, "Honey, pretty soon you're gonna be standing outside and I'll be sitting right there where you are now." And so it was,

Berlin, Potsdamer Platz circa 1930

eventually. By 1933, my mother, because she was Jewish, was unemployed and on welfare, looking for work.

Suddenly, everything started changing quickly. I had been a member of the Young Communists in Berlin-Schmargendorf. Various groups had opened up temporary soup kitchens all over the city for the millions who were unemployed and had nothing to eat. We were convinced that any moment now the *Einheitsfront*, (United Front) would take control. The United Front was made up of branches of communists, socialists, and social democrats. The Nazis called it the *mistgabel* (the "dung fork"). At night I would sit together with the other comrades in the *Rote Hilfe* ("Red Aid," a communist group) soup kitchen in Schmargendorf, practically waiting for the order to begin an armed revolt. I was almost eighteen then and in my boundless naiveté I'd say things like, "Tonight the communists strike back!" But there would be no revolt, armed or unarmed. There was no rebellion at all. Instead, after the Nazis seized power on January 30ᵗʰ 1933, I saw all of my comrades suddenly running around in the brown shirts of the SA. That was a shock. Soon you started seeing every policeman accompanied by an SA man and they went around together all day long on patrol, always with that slow step and always armed.

The communists collapsed much sooner than the social democrats who, at least in the beginning, had shown class-consciousness. The communists would fight for anyone though. Whether they were in the SA or with the communists, they were the same thugs. They had joined the SA primarily because they would receive boots, clothing, and food. In the end everyone joined; the communists—who had at least four million voices—the center party, and the social democrats. They all wanted to keep their positions and deep down in their slavish souls, they yearned for a boot kicking them from behind. They simply wanted to be ruled again since the Weimar Republic had been too weak for them. They wanted a *führer*, a leader, and that's just what they got. As Hitler said, "Give me twelve years and you will not recognize Germany." He kept that promise. Indeed, it became unrecognizable.

And today, to my astonishment, I read in the paper that there are Germans who want to have Upper Silesia back. Why and from whom, exactly, do they want it back? They should go get it back from their *führer*. He was the one who ruined it for them. He was the one who took over a large Germany and then left behind a small one. But who do they blame now? The Americans? Why don't they blame the Nazis? I cannot understand why Germans to this day don't blame the Nazis for their misfortune. It's just the opposite; Nazis still run around with heads held up high instead of being lynched. They were the ones who ruined Germany, utterly.

With father's help I would leave Berlin in early April 1933. There was an organization in Hamburg that prepared young people for immigration to Palestine. It was called *Hachsharah* which basically meant "preparation" and it was financed through the *Jewish Agency*. The director in Germany was Enzio Sireni, an Italian Jew who was a key leader for the Zionists and an unbelievably dynamic person. Later, during the war, he parachuted as a courier behind the Italian front and was shot by the Germans. Anyway, Father took me to Frau Kimmel at the Palestine Office on 10 Meineckestrasse to make the arrangements. A sign still hangs there today. If there was ever a time in my life that I was in the right place at the right time, it was at 10 Meineckestrasse on that day.

Only individuals with an immigration certificate issued by the British mandate government to the Jewish Agency were allowed to enter Palestine. The British, trying to keep a favorable impression with the Arabs, assured them there wouldn't be too many Jewish immigrants entering the country. A restrictive quota was put in place. The Zionists were interested in bringing young, able-bodied people to Palestine, capable of building up the country. They highly preferred young tradesmen and craftsmen with a pioneering spirit over doctors and lawyers. Accordingly, immigration certificates were only given to those who had some formal training in a trade. Carpenters, field workers, mechanics, bricklayers, and masons were sought. There was also the option of purchasing what were called "capitalist certificates," where you bought your visa for Palestine if you didn't have one of the skills in demand. The price of 1000 pounds sterling, however, was the equivalent of 12,000 reichmarks, and—contrary to Nazi claims—not all Jews were millionaires. Most were poor and didn't know what they were going to do. Which country would take them? Most of those who could have bought themselves visas just sent their children away and stayed home sitting on their money waiting for better times. They simply did not realize the danger that was at hand. They all kept making rationalizations up until it was too late. The German Jews told themselves that it was really the Eastern European Jews who were in trouble, not them. And when German Jewish doctors suddenly were no longer allowed to work, the Polish Jews said, "But nothing will happen to us. After all, we have a Polish passport." Everyone always believed it was someone else who was in truly in danger.

They say that you don't need to worry about protection when you know the right people, and my father knew the right people. By chance a training post had opened up in Hamburg, and Sireni asked me if I'd be prepared to start the very next day. I went home and said, "Mother, tomorrow I'm going to Hamburg." She was overjoyed. In contrast to most of the Jews, she had a keen awareness of the political climate and understood that Hitler spelled the end for us in Germany. After losing her job, she received unemployment assistance, as after all, *ordnung, or* "order," is at the heart of Germany. Now she stood on the other side of the counter. Like Tucholsky once said: The German ideal— to sit behind a counter. The German fate—to stand in front of a counter. Mother carried her fate with composure and from then on looked after older Jewish people whose children had already immigrated.

My Aunt Rosel fled to Denmark. She had to give her entire fortune to a Dane for him to marry her. He was one of these fine folks who made a profit exploiting the misfortune of Jews. He would marry a Jew, get divorced, and then marry the next one. Mr. Christensen, was his name, a professional husband. He even got my grandfather's golden pocket watch out of her. Aunt Rosel died Rosa Christensen in Sweden. There were lots of women later running around named Christensen.

Father had to disappear overnight due to his political involvement, which had put him in great danger. He took refuge in Switzerland staying a while with his friend Hermann Hesse. But before this for my 18th birthday on March 29, 1933 we had a huge birthday bash at my mother's home. That was the last time I saw him. He came back one more time in 1934 to take care of some things, which was absolutely crazy because the Gestapo was already looking for him. I was also interrogated in Hamburg because of him. He stopped by my mother's place and she nearly died when she saw him. On the way to his own place, he bumped into an actor colleague who told him that an entire year's salary of his was waiting for him at the theater where he was still officially employed. The Germans were so orderly and Prussian—a contract remains a contract, even with a warrant out for his arrest. My father actually had the gall to go back to the theater and get his pay. With that he then went to the airport and boarded the next plane to Switzerland. By midday the Gestapo had appeared at my mother's apartment looking for him.

Despite his famous friends, he could not obtain permission to reside in Switzerland. The Swiss response to exiles from Germany was hardly a model of compassion. They even let Joseph Schmidt, the famous Jewish opera tenor, die in one of their refugee camps.[1]

My father went next to Poland. In Warsaw he put together a Yiddish theatre group. In the piece "The Yellow Patch"—*Die gelle Latte* in Yiddish—by Friedrich Wolf he played Professor Mamlock. It was a hit. At the time, he wrote Lotte Lieven, "Today Dr. Wolf made a surprise appearance at the rehearsal, accompanied by his sons. They are on their way to Moscow. His son Konrad wants to become a director and the other, Markus, an actor." Konrad Wolf did indeed become a director, and Markus Wolf something rather similar, specifically, Chief of Secret Police in the former East Germany.[2]

To three million Jews living in Poland then, Alexander Granach was something of a hero, as one of their own who had made it big in Germany. In 1935 he received an invitation to the Kiev Yiddish Theater and also acted in several films shot in Russia, which I've never seen. He played a gypsy in one of them entitled, "The Last Camp." In 1936 the *saeuberungs prozesse*, the political terror in Russia started by Stalin, got under way, and in 1937 my father was arrested, not for political reasons but for "*unsolide lebenswandels*"– "improper moral conduct." The communists were not only completely humorless, but also dreadfully puritanical. Maybe that's why it was so hard to take.

A very interesting mix of people were turning up in Russia at that time: Piscator was there trying to build a German theater in the town of Engels, of all places, from which the entire German minority population was later deported. Brecht was also in Russia then, as was the actress Carola Neher, who unfortunately paid for that with her life.[3] The majority of German communists did not come out of Russia alive.

Father, however, was lucky here once again: Lion Feuchtwanger[4] along with Molotov's[5] wife, who was Jewish, tried to pull some strings for him with Stalin. They wrote a letter to Stalin, explaining that Alexander Granach was a renowned actor and his arrest was going to cast Russia in a negative light. It is the wish of everyone involved in some dirty business that their reputation won't suffer from it. As a result of this letter, my father was released from custody. One year later he visited Lion Feuchtwanger in Hollywood and fell on his knees before him. As this was happening, Martha Feuchtwanger came into the room and said, "What's going on here?" Granach gestured towards her husband and said, "This is the man who saved my life. I gather you are married to him." Mar-

Alexander Granach

tha Feuchtwanger told me this story when I met her in America, long after the war.

My father left Russia for Switzerland where he performed in "Macbeth" and "Danton" at the Zurich Schauspielhaus. In the spring of 1938, he traveled aboard one of the very last ships from Lisbon to New York. He arrived in America on the 14th of May, without means and knowing not a word of English. He located his brothers and sisters who had immigrated to the U.S. from Galicia in the 1920s and had tried their luck with little result since then. Even his elderly mother was living in America then. They all lived on the Lower East Side and had nothing. In contrast to those who fit the stereotype of having "a rich uncle in America," my father had to support himself and his youngest brother. He lived in one of those tenement houses and had to learn English fast, which apparently was rather difficult for him. During this period he began to write his memoirs.

In New York he met up with Leopold Jessner and together they decided to start a German theater. They gave a performance of *Wilhelm Tell*. It wasn't exactly the sort of thing all America had been waiting for, William Tell performed by German actors in German.

Some of the first anti-Nazi films were starting to be produced in Los Angeles, so my father headed out there along with his youngest brother. Actors with German accents were in demand to play SS members, and these turned out to be almost exclusively Jewish actors from Germany who had fled the Nazis. Ironically, they put on SS uniforms and were shouting and otherwise behaving how American film directors imagined the Nazis to be. Or they played Gestapo agents and, for reasons beyond me, often wore bowler hats.

In 1973 I was invited to an exhibition opening at the Berlin Academy of Arts. The theme was "German Theater in Exile." An opening speech was given by a certain Herr Trebitsch, who was once something like Max Reinhardt's right hand man. He remarked that in two thousand years, archaeologists would probably discover reels of film, and come across the old American anti-Nazi films. People will see these Jewish actors and say, "Yes, those were the Nazis and that is how they must have looked...”! But at least an actor could make a living in Hollywood with these roles, and my father certainly did. His career blossomed again and he went around with money, had a large circle of friends, and had his affairs. I know about all this from my cousin who lived with him.

Many of father's old friends from Berlin had come to Hollywood. Bert Brecht worked as a screenwriter. He wrote *Hangmen also Die* and Fritz Lang directed it. Billy Wilder was there. Marlene Dietrich was there, and Elisabeth Bergner too. Ernst Lubitsch had already established himself. Because it was clear that there was no audience in America for the kind of thing that Alfred Polgar[6] wrote, he was put up in a room and more or less told not to write anything. Doeblin[7] wasn't doing any better. Hollywood was simply not the right place for German intelligentsia. Most had a hard time making it in America. Lacking a language was particularly difficult for the actors, and the more famous they had been in Germany, the harder it was for them to make the transition to America. There is nothing quite so tragic as an actor without a language. An author can write. A singer can sing in any language. But an actor becomes voiceless.

My father never had any of the pretentiousness that many stars do, and perhaps that's why he was able to adjust in America. He had some leading roles but also many smaller ones that he was happy to receive, such as in the film *1914–The Last Days Before the War* with Heinrich George in the lead role. An awful film. In it George says, "I'm going to write a book on war and peace..." as he raises a spoonful of soup to his mouth. Suddenly a shot is heard and George's face falls into the soup. Then Granach comes forward out of the crowd of shocked bystanders and delivers the extremely important line, "Juares is dead! He wanted peace..." They spoke very slowly in films back then so even those sitting in the back rows could understand what was going on. There was also the never-ending handshake in *Comradeship* that my father gave. Some directors treated the public like they were morons.

My father's dream was to do theater in America, but preferred to do Yiddish theater only as a last resort. He did tour once with a Yiddish theater ensemble. They performed pieces on anarchy, socialism, freedom, and the ghetto. For him these were quintessential Jewish themes. The public, however, had a different idea of what Yiddish theater was. They were used to kitsch and wanted to see things like *A Chassene im Shtetl (A Wedding in Town),* where first the bride doesn't want to get married, then the groom doesn't, then the parents don't, then all of them don't, but by the end everything turns out fine and everyone is happy.

In Yiddish theater, terrible things are supposed to happen and it is the only theater in the world where the program says, "A tragedy with song and dance." Even when the piece is very dramatic, the actors come on stage at the end, hold hands and sing and dance. Sure, Yiddish theater was provincial theater, full of shouting and melodrama, but the audience was the best an actor could ever wish for. In the end, they really wanted to see the villain be vanquished and justice be done.

Although my father acted in many Hollywood films,

notably *Ninotchka* and *For Whom the Bell Tolls,* his true passion was always live theater. His big break on Broadway happened in December 1944, in *A Bell for Adano,* a wartime story set in Italy. He was performing up until his final moments when they had to take him down from the stage, rush him to the hospital, and operate on his appendix. Shortly thereafter, on the 14th of April, 1945, he died from an embolism.

Rabbi Joachim Prinz, who had been at my Bar Mitzvah, laid him to rest. He told me later that he just couldn't believe my father was dead. When he saw him on his bed at the hospital in New York he said, "All right Granach, stop fooling around. You had us for awhile but come on now, get up!" And later whenever I met Joachim Prinz somewhere, he'd say, "Gerhard, I laid your father to rest."

CHAPTER THREE

The fact that the *Hachsharah*-Center existed in Hamburg for Jewish youth bound for Palestine was like a miracle. It spared me from vanishing up the chimneys at Auschwitz. If it hadn't been for this, mother and I would have been stuck in Germany. We didn't have enough money to make it to Prague like the many others who fled, going first to Austria, then Prague, then France, and finally Holland, whereupon they were given a one-way express ride back to Auschwitz. We didn't even have the money for that.

So in June 1933, I took a night train to Hamburg, and with that, my life took a turn. I did what thousands of young Jews were doing, changing course and no longer looking to become a doctor, a lawyer, pursue a literary career, or even becoming a cameraman or an actor. It was time now to simply learn a trade and prepare oneself for life in Palestine. For us that was the only alternative.

The *Hachsharah*-Center in Hamburg was a kind of urban kibbutz. There were three of them and we lived in *Bet Chalutz*–Pioneer House–on Beneckestrasse 6. The house belonged to the Jewish community. Approximately forty boys and girls lived together there and had training posts at various German companies around Hamburg. They were working as gardeners, farm workers, painters, and brick-layers.

My job for Palestine was to build baking ovens and so I was dispensed to the Karl Ehmke firm for an internship. I was the youngest one there and always had to crawl inside the ovens to install things. For me, these were wonderful years. I was young, had a job, and all the fellow employees were nice to me even though they knew I was Jewish. When I told them that I was headed for Palestine, they attempted to talk me out of it; "But it's so hot down there. And this thing with Hitler, it'll all soon be over with. His bark is worse than his bite, you know. It'll be better if you stay here, my boy." They meant well and truly believed what they said. Later I learned to do construction, specifically plastering and brick-laying. As paradoxical as it may seem, my time in Hamburg between 1933 and 1936 was carefree and happy.

At *Bet Chalutz* we received a solid craftsman's training and built up a real Zionist *sehnsucht*, or longing. We couldn't wait to arrive in the Promised Land. We sang songs in Hebrew, learned Zionist and Jewish history, and were ready to invest all our strength in founding a Jewish state in Palestine, a place where Jews might finally find peace, and for those not living there, a base of support. That's how it is to this day. Jews can indeed live practically anywhere in the world, but when a country no longer wants them, the door to Israel is always open. There's enough space here to accommodate everyone, and we will make room for more. I mean in Israel itself, not the occupied territories. It's like how it goes sometimes with people on a bus: The ones who are already on shout, "We're full,"

Hamburg in 1935 (Gad Granach with accordian)

and want the bus doors to stay closed and to just drive on. You're standing in the middle and nobody wants to move towards the back. Everyone wants to be as close as possible to the front by the driver. Everyone is saying, "We're full!" but there's still more room, plenty more.

We were like heroes to the Hamburg Jews back then. The upper-middle class marveled at our courage, at our willingness to go into and build up this wild land. We were their future. The Hamburg Jews had invited us and were supporting us, but they themselves would never have been prepared to immigrate to Palestine. Thus the saying back then went, "A Zionist is someone who convinces a rich Jew to give his money to another Jew so that he can go to Pales-

Hamburg, 1935 (Gad Granach at far right)

tine." Of course, there were also vocal anti-Zionists, stub-born types completely convinced that Germany was where they belonged. They were the ones still wearing an iron cross on their collar when they were taken to Auschwitz, in denial until the very end.

The craziest things happened during this period in Hamburg. As *nichtarier,* "non-Aryans," we were not supposed to serve in the German *wehrmacht* but they went through all the motions of a regular call-up anyhow. I too was called up for an inspection. At the end of the process, the commanding officer asked me, "So then, which troop do you wish to join, young man?" to which I replied, "I don't want to join any troop."–"But why not, then?"–"Because I'm a non-Aryan" I said. "Oh what a load of nonsense!" he responded in frustration. Next to me stood a real giant, over seven feet tall with hands like shovels, but nevertheless a "non-Aryan." It would drive the *wehrmacht* officers crazy how such good material for cannon fodder stood right before them but they couldn't use it now. I could only be assigned to *Ersatzreserve II*, "Reserve troops II."

Unlike Berlin, the Nazi presence in Hamburg didn't feel so strong yet. We only had a bit of trouble with the local branch of Hitler Youths that always wanted to raid our hostel at night. There were at least forty of us in the same place, which for them was real convenient. It was utterly pointless explaining to them that we were leaving soon anyway, they just wanted to fight. We were lucky that one of us was an expert in jiu-jitsu and he once gave a small gang of Hitler Youth such a beating that they never bothered us again.

The *Hachsharah* was wonderful except for the Zionist meetings we were supposed to attend. I never did go to any of those meetings. I'd already had my fill of political slogans back in the Communist Youth Movement. By this time I knew the distinction between theory and practice very well. Even with the communists, I never did believe in a proletarian dictatorship. Government should be left to the intelligentsia, people with knowledge and character, and not to apparatchiks who sit on their jobs simply by virtue of their fat asses. And that's how it was at the *Hachsharah*. To me it was clear that when we arrived in Palestine, we were going to have to work hard, and that the reality would have nothing to do with our dreams and theories. Even at that time, there was unrest between Jews

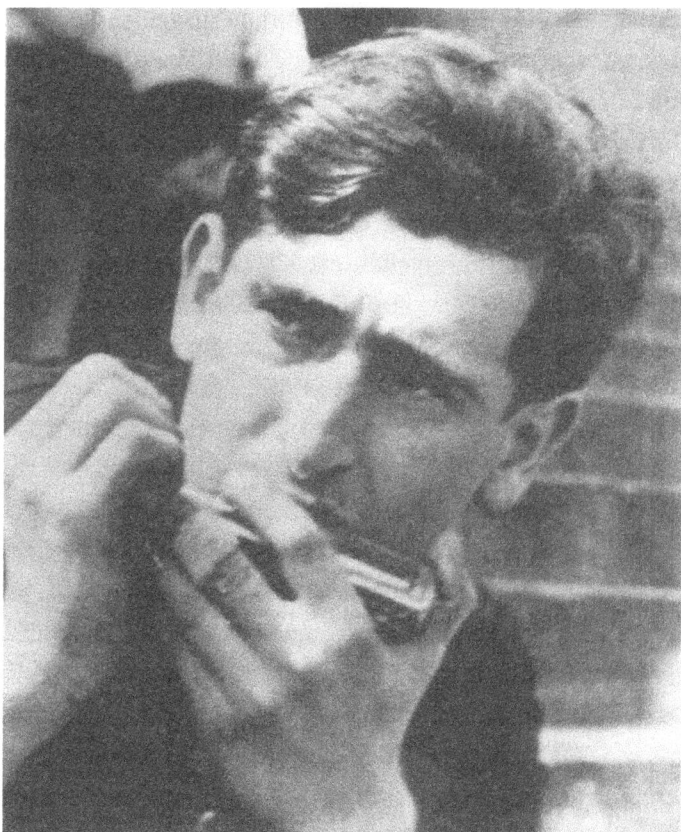

At Jewish sport festival in Bremen

and Arabs. I was keenly aware that things would come to a head and then all that theoretical stuff wasn't going to help us a bit.

Due to my attitude, they categorized me for a long time as "Zionistically immature." They discovered that I hadn't been attending Hebrew classes regularly either. I had a very hard time with Hebrew. The local dialect *platt-*

deutsch, however, I picked up right away, but that wasn't going to do me much good in Palestine. After three years I made it clear to them that even though I might not be the most died-in-the-wool Zionist, I was nonetheless a fine bricklayer. In the end, I was declared sufficiently worthy of being sent to Palestine and finally got my immigration certificate. That was in 1936, and not a moment too soon.

I went to Berlin, packed my bags, and said goodbye to mother at Lehrter station. We both knew that it might be forever, as we had no idea how she was going to make it to Palestine. Still she was brave, and happy that at least I would make it out of Germany. She was one of the few people who saw the writing on the wall, and thanks to her, I got out in time. An entire train was packed with young people like myself who possessed the *arbeitszertifikat* (work permit). Their families stood on the platform. There must have been a thousand people there, saying their good-byes and weeping. And in the middle of it all, the train station police with their lovely comments: "Why don't you all just leave together right now? Go! Get out of here, every single one of you!" These were the last Germans we saw. A foul group. They made the act of leaving very easy for us.

Ⅰt was high time the Jewish people endeavored to achieve something solely for their own benefit, and cease intervening in the struggles of other nations on their behalf. They were involved everywhere—but what was it all for in the end? During the Russian Revolution, Jews were at the forefront, and did this prove any help to them in the end? And Rosa Luxemburg[1], was it necessary that she die fighting for the German worker? As if German workers really wanted a revolution! They wanted to have their old Kaiser back again, but Rosa Luxemburg gave her life fighting for their rights. And the shooting of Walter Rathenau[2]...what was it all for? Personally, it angers me. It truly does. The Jews never did something solely for their own kind, yet if all these great minds had come together just for their people, there's nothing they couldn't have achieved. Perhaps even here today, things would look different in Israel.

On the way from Triest to Palestine, we conducted ourselves exactly as we had been instructed to according to the Zionist plan: to be full of enthusiasm. We danced and celebrated through the night. At one point an instructor came up to us and said, "How can you dance when Jewish blood is being spilled in Palestine?" I said, "That's exactly why I want to dance one more time!" At daybreak we could see the silhouette of Haifa and became very excited. We reached the port of *Eretz Yisrael* around six in the morning on a June day in 1936. At first I thought we had arrived at the wrong wedding—the harbor was full of Haurani laborers running around in their brightly colored clothes and blue painted eyes.[3] All of them looked like Ghengis Khan to me. I overheard a distinguished looking German Jew say to his son, "Herbert, I think we've arrived ten years too early."

We were loaded right away onto buses and taken to a new immigrants hostel. From now on we were *chalut-*

The harbor in Haifa

Arab harbor police

zim, pioneers. I remember how I immediately went into town to buy some new clothes. Under no circumstances did I want to be seen going around in my German winter clothes, from which everyone could instantly tell that I had just arrived. I bought some khaki pants, a khaki shirt, and a safari pith helmet, but when I came back to the hostel, they all laughed. Afterwards, the safari helmet just sat atop my dresser in the kibbutz.

Eventually we met up with our old comrades from the *Hachsharah* who had already been in Palestine for some time. They had all suddenly forgotten their German and now only spoke Hebrew amongst themselves, which naturally made a big impression on us. Today, however, I know they couldn't really speak Hebrew yet. It was just a show to impress us and make us feel a bit inferior and miserable.

A few weeks later we were placed on Kibbutz Shfayim. At Shfayim there were one hundred and fifty Poles, Russians, and Latvians who'd been living there since 1933. Real culture shock suddenly hit us then. We would've preferred living on a kibbutz with people from Germany whom we already knew. Apparently that wasn't an option. Instead the authorities from the kibbutz movement decided to try an experiment with us. They already knew Western Jews could live together well with *sabras*, native born Jews. Now they wanted to see how West European Jews and East European Jews would get along together on the same kibbutz. Shfayim was one of the poorest kibbutzim in the entire country with very little land or property and dependent upon outside work. And now we, new immigrants from Germany, were to join them.

When we first arrived, there was barely a kibbutz to be seen. There were no buildings with the exception of a brick house for the children. The adults lived in tents and barracks. The first thing Jewish immigrants did when they came to the country was plant trees. A few years ago, an Egyptian journalist coming to visit me drove across the country. She remarked, "It's interesting how the Jews have settled in all the nicest areas." I could not believe my ears. The woman simply had no clue. When I came to Shfayim in 1936, the place was bare as an ass. We planted the first trees there. I remember well how on *Tu Bishevat*, the Jewish Festival of Trees in spring, we lined the first avenue of the kibbutz with frail young trees. Now, fifty years later, a journalist from Egypt comes here and says, "Interesting how the Jews have settled in all the nicest areas." We were always sold only the worst pieces of land, nothing but rocky desert and marshlands, but we did the best we could with it. I am not much of a Zionist, but that we built up and planted on the land is simply a fact.

Today Shfayim is a flourishing kibbutz about a half-hour away from Tel Aviv. Back then there wasn't even a road to speak of connecting them. The road ended in Herzliya and then you had to walk miles on foot along dirt trails and tracks left behind by trucks and other vehicles. In the beginning all of those things were so new and exciting to us that we weren't too bothered. Only later did it really sink in that we weren't in Hamburg anymore. The colloquial language on the kibbutz was Yiddish, so that's what I learned instead of Hebrew. Frankly speaking, it was much easier. When someone at work would address me in Hebrew, I'd always say, "*Chaver*, speak Yiddish!" To work under a blazing hot sun and have to speak Hebrew at the same time was just too much. Yiddish, however, came almost without trying. As they say, "one speaks Hebrew, but Yiddish speaks all by itself."

From my very first day in Palestine until the present, there has always been something happening, something going on here. Arab unrest was occurring already by 1936. Not until 1939 when the British stopped allowing more Jews to enter did things calm down. Up until then you could hear gunshots every night. The *Ghaffirim*, young Jewish auxiliary police who carried arms, made a real impression on me. They were the first armed Jews I had seen in my life! After two weeks I too became a *Ghaffir*. That, however, would be the last time that I enlisted voluntarily for anything.

The *Ghaffirim* were organized by the Jewish Agency, but subordinate to the British Palestine Police. The British though, were not particularly interested in showing us too much. We basically just learned useless military drills from them: standing at attention, marching, rifle over the shoulder, and other nonsense. Soon we were performing the drills so well that we could have been in the British Royal Guard. Our superiors wanted us to win the trophy in the annual drill competition which was completely *meshugge*. The most absurd part was that the commands were given in English, which almost none of us understood. We just responded to the intonations like trained dogs. Since I was the only one who knew some English, everybody looked at me to see what to do. When the command from up front was "right!" and I inadvertently went left, then so did everybody else.

For the competition they had us marching around a tennis court. One Jewish so-called sergeant was trying to show off a little by ordering his men to throw themselves on the ground. Unfortunately, he forgot the English command for "stand up." As our squad marched by he asked us in Yiddish how to say it but our commander said to keep our mouths shut. We won the trophy and they are probably still lying there today. It was all very comical but they re-

With reserve police in Palestine, 1936
Top: 3rd from right; Bottom 2nd from left

ally should have had us doing something more useful.

Our *ghaffir* uniforms were half-English, half-Turkish and for headgear, fur hats. This looked very chic and romantic to us. Some of us even rode on horses. But the romanticism was not to last. Shfayim was surrounded by a no-man's land. The Arabs planted land mines at night and were constantly shooting at us from their neighboring village. Every night we had to stay in concrete bunkers and keep watch. This was not how we imagined being saved from the Nazis would be.

Life in general wasn't easy for us in the beginning. Fortunately, there was a group of twenty-five of us from Hamburg together and we could help each other out. We weren't homesick whatsoever, not for a second, just the opposite actually. We were damn happy to have gotten away from Germany. Naturally, though, we couldn't forget Germany, with our suitcases full of German books and German culture. Later we found those books in the rooms of the Polish. They had their pillows sitting up on their beds with a sharp kink in the middle. I wondered all the time how they managed to get the pillows to stay like that. I looked underneath them one day and found Schiller, Goethe, and Heine, propping them up.

There was a constant tension between the Jews from Eastern Europe and us German Jews. The cultural gap was huge. Our living habits differed, we dressed differently, ate differently, and furnished our rooms differently. The East European Jews looked down upon us even while we made fun of them. Naturally we thought of ourselves as more intelligent than them and culturally superior. The

Poles would say, and they were completely correct, "You and your culture! Where has it got you now? What is left for you from your Goethe?"

Evenings we would sit in the common room and read the paper. Back then "Davar" was the only Hebrew newspaper. It was torn into four separate pieces so more people could read it at the same time. One day, just as the papers arrived with fresh news form Germany, someone came up to me and said, "Here, look what *your* Hitler is doing!" In Germany I was a dirty Jew, and now here, suddenly, I was a representative of the Greater German Reich. *My* Hitler? Sometimes we came to blows. *Yekke-potz* was a frequently hurled insult. There was a joke then, about the child of German Jewish parents who comes home from school one day and says, "They all tell me I'm the child of a '*yekke-potz.*' What's that supposed to mean?" "I'll tell you exactly what it means," says the father. "*Yekke*4, because we came from Germany, and *potz* because we stayed here."

At Shfayim you could instantly distinguish a room belonging to an East European Jew from one belonging to a *yekke*. In the Poles' rooms everything was always stark white and orderly, but in ours it was colorful and cozy. We hung prints of our favorite painters, the sunflowers of van Gogh, the horses of Marc, the works of Klee and Picasso, and Modigliani nudes with their long necks and broad thighs. They didn't care for our tastes at all, and we found theirs impossible. They hung rugs on their walls bought in the bazaar, portraying Jerusalem at sunset with David's Tower in the background and two camels up front. On the bottom was written "Yerushalayim." Tucholsky once said,

"It's very good when an ashtray has 'ashtray' written on it, otherwise one just might mistake it for a crocodile."

And then there was the food. Kibbutz food was simply awful. First of all, there were no potatoes because they had the fixed belief that potatoes wouldn't grow on our kibbutz. Instead we had tons of bread because the East European Jews ate bread with everything. All their delicacies from home landed on our table; milk soup with herring for example, an impossible combination that would have made better prison food. Then there was *schwarze kasche*, which is buckwheat porridge and stinks like an old dresser drawer that hasn't been opened in years. *Schwarze kasche* is really something unspeakably awful. Whosoever can consume that, had to have been born in Eastern Europe.

The culture war raged on all sides. We couldn't believe what the Polish would eat and they in turn found the way we ate very amusing. They didn't understand why we chewed our food with closed mouths, and they would do imitations mocking and making fun of us. "Those *yekkes*!" they'd say while demonstratively chewing with their mouths closed. They thought it was so silly; you're not supposed to eat like that. One eats with an open mouth of course! And noisily too, smacking the lips so the world can see that it tastes good.

Our staple food was eggplant, or in Hebrew *chatzilim*. Out of *chatzilim* you can make almost anything, except maybe new soles for your shoes. We ate *chatzilim* until it grew out of our ears. They made *chatzilim* steaks and *chatzilim* schnitzel. They made chopped liver from *chatzilim*. They made stewed fruit salad from *chatzilim* and turned it into a sour appetizer. They made *chatzilim* goulash and served it both hot and cold. And the regular *chatzilim* salad made from the innermost part, it looked so gray, just like cement. At night we dreamt of *chatzilim*. When they made a marmalade spread out of *chatzilim*, that was really the last straw. It was enough to drive you nuts. You would wake up every morning, go to the breakfast hall, and then there it was, waiting for you on your plate. Already that was enough for the entire day. And people wonder now why I'm not particularly keen on eggplant.

If you fell ill on the kibbutz and went to the hospital, you received a hard-boiled egg to eat in addition to the inescapable eggplant. It made no difference why someone was in the hospital—whether it was for an upset stomach, a bro-

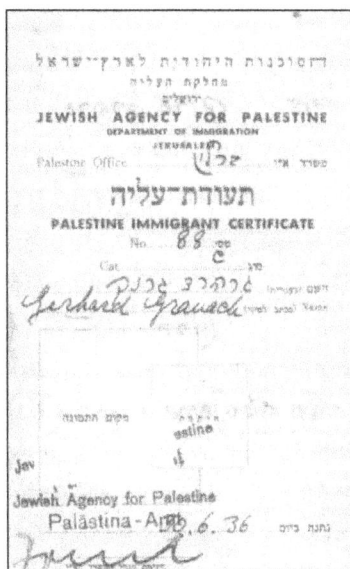

Certificate of immigration
June 30th, 1936

ken hand, or fresh from an operation—no matter, an egg was always served, eggs boiled at five in the morning so, God forbid, you wouldn't get too greedy and think of actually eating a warm, soft egg. No, it was always hard-boiled and it would stick in your throat. Some people preferred not to eat theirs right away, instead tucking it in their shirt pocket and saving it for later. They probably became speculators later of some kind. At the next meal when nobody else had one they would take it out and set it on the table. Everyone would just stare.

I recall someone saving an egg in his pocket, one that turned out not to be completely hard-boiled. I remember who it was; it was Chanan Hershkowitz. We were working outside in the orange groves and Chanan was saving his for lunch. On a large table sat bread and more oranges for us, as if we hadn't had enough of them while working. Chanan was feeling sort of special, knowing he had an egg to go with his meal, but as he felt in his shirt pocket, he realized what had happened. Nobody said a word, but everyone saw the yellow fingers come up, and they were silently pleased. That was God's punishment.

With the girls on the kibbutz we also had our troubles. They behaved very differently here than those in Germany. In Germany, when a girl lets you kiss her, you knew where you stood. With the Polish girls, however, they might go into the hay with you and start kissing and fooling around, but then they always draw the line at the waist. From the waist down, they became very moral.

Since the Polish are excellent tailors we made everything

At Kibbutz Shfayim 1937

for ourselves in the tailor-shop, even bras. These were laced up from the back and were proper armored devices with double stitched pointy cups on which could practically poke your eye out. The girls sometimes wore laced bodices and to undo them, one needed a mechanic. I was always afraid my hand would get stuck back there and I'd never get it out.

On the kibbutz, being married certainly had its advantages. If your wife became pregnant, it was like paradise on earth. First of all, you could partake of the better food your wife received from the kitchen. Pregnant wives, you see, were given a quarter chicken every single day. I'm still surprised that the children didn't come out looking like chickens. A quarter chicken, each day, doubly dead; slaughtered, then boiled to death. We watched the married men with envy sitting next to their pale wives with their paler chickens, finishing up what they couldn't, or wouldn't, eat. Not only did they get the chicken, they even received their own private room as a couple. The rest of us, the unmarried, were living four to a room and had no privacy, not to mention any real love life. Our love life occurred behind the stables, so to speak. We were indeed young, but one didn't always want to do it standing up. It would have been nice to have had it with some degree of comfort now and again, but marriage was the only way to for that.

The marriage process went like this: First you went to the *mazkir*, the kibbutz secretary and said: I am together with Chana, Chava, Rachel, or whomever. Then you could get a *chedar mishpacha*, a family or couple's room. They made a cake in the kitchen for you, wrote *Mazel Tov* across it, and that was it. Once a year the rabbi came to Shfayim and went around non-stop performing circumcisions and other services. He wouldn't eat with us, however. The kibbutz, after all, was not kosher.

I was with a girl in a *chedar mishpacha* for two years. One day as I was coming back from work–I was an auxiliary policeman then and remember well how we were shot at on the way home– all my belongings were strewn across the grass in front of our room. She had thrown me out, but that's another story.

In the beginning when there wasn't enough housing in place yet, even married couples had to share their rooms with a third person. They used to call this person a "primus." This, actually, was what the stove was called that stood in the corner for boiling water. In truth, it really wasn't necessary to put a "primus" in the room, even during the housing shortage, but the whole kibbutz was full of such unnecessary annoyances. One was supposed to live a rough life on principle. There was this notion that building up a new land was supposed to be a rough and rugged affair. If they had stuck a few nails in our beds we would've put up with that too. But really, the discrimination against the unmarried was outrageous. Eventually I became fed up with working for other people. I was slaving away while they were making babies.

I performed practically every job imaginable: roofing, glazing, pouring concrete, and of course bricklaying and plastering. With these particular skills, I was in fact rather in demand in Palestine. The many academics coming from Germany then—the lawyers, scientists, and doctors—they had a much more difficult time finding work. There's a fitting story here from this period: A bus with thirty people was driving through an orange plantation when suddenly one of the passengers falls unconscious from the extreme heat. The bus driver pulls over and twenty-nine people jump up shouting, "I'm a doctor! I'm a doctor!" Then the bus driver says, "Quiet Gentlemen! This is my patient!" That's really how it was. Academic folks were not so highly regarded; they could barely make a living. The bus drivers were the real aristocrats in Palestine back then. After them, came the masons.

I had a cousin here who used to date a bus driver—and that was considered something at the time! Bus drivers, by the way, were often the children of wealthy parents. Though they weren't able to make it out of Germany with all their money, but they did succeed in bringing other

Working the fields on the kibbutz

things over. They bought themselves a bus or car in Germany and brought it to Palestine. In Haifa, every bus line belonged to a different cooperative recognizable by their separate colors. The #4 bus drove up the hill where the well-to-do people lived, and the #4 drivers themselves were well-to-do too. All the drivers imitated the English way, wearing nicely pressed khaki shirts and khaki shorts with wool stockings and a pipe stuck down the side. Many bus cooperatives and taxi companies were founded by *yekkes*.

Back then I also led caravans of camels for a time. Kibbutz Shfayim was about a half mile from the Mediterranean Sea and the beach belonged to us. Sand was scraped together from the beach, loaded onto camels, and then brought to the construction sites. We owned twelve camels bought from Arabs in Be'er Sheva. They woul never sell us the females, so we wouldn't be able to breed them ourselves.

It wasn't an easy life, yet it was an exciting and free one. Each day was interesting. Perhaps it sounds cynical but sometimes I thought to myself that I had Hitler to thank for everything. For just that reason we sometimes called him the *herführer*, the "over-here-leader"[5,] because he led us to coming here in a sense. We didn't feel homesickness or any real longing for Germany, maybe just a bit for the European weather, to see a few clouds in the sky during summer. The eternal bright blue sky here can start to get on one's nerves just as much as the perpetually gray skies over Germany do. Or similarly, to see a real dark and dense forest again, not like the ones we have with just a few dusty trees. The Germans, in contrast, long for the sun. One always wishes for what one does not have.

My mother came in 1937. I was very fortunate in obtaining immigration papers for her, which was no easy task back then when the emphasis was on bringing young people into the country. It wasn't that the elderly were simply being written off, yet neither was it a coincidence that a Yiddish song from the kibbutz went,

Tate und Mama, laengst schon vergessen ("Father and mother, long since forgotten"). Oh how I hated hearing that song.

Mother was extremely happy to be out of Germany. Two of her sisters, Aunt Hedel and Aunt Emma wouldn't make it, their lives ending in the Lodz Ghetto like so many other Berlin Jews. At the time though, we didn't have the slightest clue of what awaited them.

Aunt Johanna, my mother's older sister, came to Palestine in 1935. She was a housekeeper for an attorney from Breslau by the name of Nothmann. We called him "RA" for short, the abbreviation for attorney (*rechtsanwalt*) in German. They left Germany together. He had a little chicken farm, which was more of a hobby than a business. For him it was a way of satisfying his Zionist ambitions and doing his part in building the country, all in a very *yekke*-like manner. RA was divorced, and my aunt was a widow. Even though they spent the rest of their lives together, they never stopped addressing each other formally. He called her *Frau Meier* and she referred to him similarly as *Herr Rechtsanwalt*, "Mr. Attorney," both in Breslau and by the chicken coops in Rishon Letzion.

I used to visit Aunt Johanna frequently. Anyone living on a kibbutz back then was always glad to visit relatives, hoping that at least they might get something decent to eat. My aunt would serve the meal in the dining room and everything was very refined. RA had old inherited furniture from Germany in their home. Even though they didn't need the egg business for their livelihood, they took it all

Kibbutz Shfayim 1937

At Kibbutz Shfayim 1939

very seriously. Each time I came they were sitting in the kitchen counting all their eggs. There was a scale to weigh them and a large book in which each individual egg was recorded. Non-stop the eggs were washed, weighed, recorded, and packed. They were busy the whole day with this operation. They also kept a donkey in the stables and RA wore a big straw hat. Rishon Letzion wasn't very developed then but it did have roads. In the afternoon he would ride his donkey wearing that straw hat down Herzl Avenue and cut the best grass from the side of the road for his chickens.

My mother worked for the Rosenblums then who had family in Switzerland. One day they received a small tin of *Nescafé Instant Coffee* from Switzerland which had just come out and was very popular. This was in the early 1940s. The Rosenblums gave it to my mother, but since she was an extremely modest woman she could not allow herself to open it, so she decided to give it to her sister. She took the bus down to Rishon Letzion—not a particularly easy journey as we were in the middle of a war—to bring her sister the container of Nescafé. Johanna, likewise, was a very modest woman and was just as unlikely to open it as my mother. So she placed it upon the house altar, that is, on top of the radio for all visitors to see.

In those days, the radio was the absolute center of attention in the home. Everyone would sit around it to hear the latest news about the war. *Radio Hilversum* was a major broadcast station then. When someone paid Aunt Johanna a visit, they were told about the priceless object atop the radio, but nobody actually ventured to open it. In Rishon

Letzion at the time, there were lots of anniversaries, bar mitzvahs, and birthdays, and on one such occasion Aunt Johanna gave the tin of Nescafé as a gift. The proud recipients placed it atop of their radio and eventually gave it away again one day. It had become a wandering prize and everywhere it went, it was set atop the radio and no one ever opened it—they probably didn't even know how to! At any rate, it traveled around town for a year and a half until it finally arrived back at my aunt's, again as a gift, of course. As they say, "How small Rishon Letzion is."

Aunt Johanna lived to be ninety-one. At one time when she wasn't feeling well she visited a hospital in Jerusalem. The hospital on Jaffa Street was called Shaarey Tzedek and was founded in 1866 by a *yekke* doctor. It was not, however, a proper modern hospital. It was more like a museum with large halls and old-fashioned furniture, as if nothing had changed since the day it opened in 1866. If Aunt Johanna hadn't fallen off the narrow bed in that hospital, she might still be alive today.

By 1938, more and more illegal refugees were arriving from Europe. Officially only 55,000 Jews were to be allowed into Palestine, children included. The British would not allow any more than this. With our kibbutz situated along the shoreline, it became a kind of landing point. Often when we came home from work we'd find a note on our beds telling us to be at a certain time at a certain place on the kibbutz. A car would then drive up, which was in itself quite a rarity, and drop off a radio transmitter that would later guide the ship to a particular point. Around midnight a simple stable lamp was put up on the beach so the captain could see where the ship was to drop anchor. Most ships were a poor excuse for sea-worthy vessels. People used to call them *seelenverkaeufer*, "sold soul ships." It was a life-endangering affair to travel aboard such pieces of junk. But everything in life is relative, including danger. Rifles were distributed among us and we positioned lookouts around the area, keeping watch to make sure no Bedouins with camels wandered by, and above all, to keep the British from getting involved.

Then the ships would arrive. They were small Greek coastal ships with 200, 300, sometimes 400 people at most. The really large vessels weren't used until much later. Men from the "Workers Rowing Club" out of Tel Aviv were waiting for them in rowboats. They rowed up close to the ships and people climbed down with their bundles into the rowboats. The crew, however, had to be taken ashore first. We learned that the hard way. The first time they simply took the money, tossed the refugees and their bundles into the water, and took off. Since then the rule was: Nobody gets paid until the last person is safely handed over to us.

The rowboats went non-stop back and forth bringing people ashore. The new arrivals couldn't believe their luck and would fall to their knees on the sand to kiss the ground. They finally had their freedom and saw, for the first time, Jews standing at the better end of a rifle, namely behind the butt instead of looking into its barrel. Then we'd load their things onto camels and head toward the road where buses stood were waiting for them. By five in the morning there would be no trace of the ship or the new immigrants.

The British police never did get in our way because, oddly enough, they were always celebrating a birthday with one of the Jewish police reservists in the next village. There were a conspicuously large number of birthdays back then to celebrate, and I think the British might also have known what all these birthdays were about.

Then the war began overseas. There was no longer contact with Europe, no mail, no signs of life, just vague reports of Jews being persecuted. People suspected much more than what was actually known, especially among the people from Eastern Europe who were extremely worried about their relatives.

$\mathbf{B}$y 1944, I'd had enough of living and working on the kibbutz. I held out for eight years and it was time to move on. I desired to leave sooner, and I wasn't the only one, but it wasn't easy to leave the others. If you did go, you were seen as a traitor. They would try to frighten you out of it, saying that life outside the kibbutz was a jungle, and that the real aristocrats and builders of the country were us, the *kibbutzniks*. Ultimately, we had allowed ourselves to be exploited, not simply for money, but for Zionism. Once it became known that you were going to leave, then you soon found yourself sitting alone in the dining hall—no one would join you.

I'd been doing work for the kibbutz down at the Dead Sea since 1940, something I volunteered to do, not because the pioneering spirit seized me, but because my friend Ossi from Hamburg wanted to go there. Our work brought in good money for the kibbutz and we had a wonderful time far away from the rest of the world. Today it takes only forty minutes to travel from Jerusalem to the Dead Sea, but back then you had to leave at the crack of dawn to get there by nine at night. The Dead Sea is about 50 miles long and our camp was at the southern tip, in Sodom. Accessible only by boat, it took eight hours to get there. By the time newspapers reached us down there, they were usually quite old.

The Dead Sea is a world unto itself, 400 meters below sea level. You feel like you've plunged into a warm *fruchtsuppe*. Everything feels sugary and not quite real. One sees the water, the mountains, the vast expanse, yet somehow still has a feeling of being closed in. Sound also seems to travel further down there. At first I felt as if the Dead Sea was a forbidden land, so quiet and otherworldly. You could sense the minerals escaping from the Sea; bromine for example, which had a very calming effect.[1] The scenery was fantastic but the heat was unbearable. I worked as a locomotive driver on a small railway transporting potash from the harbor back to a work site. It was a German loco-

Locomotive by the Dead Sea

motive made by Ohrenstein and Koppel. Due to the war, replacement parts were impossible to get and we had to improvise. We even cast new cylinders ourselves. From our experience on the kibbutz we had become accustomed to figuring out a way to help ourselves in any situation.

Working the afternoon shift in the heat of the day, I had to hop on the locomotive without using my hands because you'd get burned if you touched the hand-rails. 112-degree sunshine is bearable, but hot iron at that temperature isn't. You had to be careful as hell not to burn yourself. Because the work was so demanding we were fed much more and better fare than on the kibbutz, just the opposite of what we were used to. At the Dead Sea we had meat twice a day as well as eggs in the morning for breakfast, and that was in the middle of a war when everything was rationed! We also did a little bit of private business on the side with the Bedouins from Transjordan, so we were living rather well. Our thoughts revolved mostly around which shift we had, what there was to eat, and of course girls. Of the one hundred young people sent from the kibbutz to the Dead Sea, one third were girls and the others were boys, all unmarried of course. By and large, those who ended up there were the more adventurous or crazy types. Every four weeks we had a break and traveled back to the home kibbutz.

The night shift began at around eight in the evening and finished at five in the morning. Afterwards, the whole day was free. We had a garden, a kiosk with newspapers, a bar, and we'd all just hang around. The girls worked in the kitchen so it was difficult to get near them. If you had the

The camp in Sodom along the Dead Sea

night shift you didn't stand a chance with the girls because the competition from the day shift went out with them then. We would fight over shifts to be with them. When you finally got lucky with one, then it was soon time to go back to the home kibbutz again. Later, when you returned to the camp, a single look at the locomotive driver was all it took for you to know. He would just shake his head and say, "Forget about her. She's going out with 'so-and-so' now." These were our main troubles.

The Palestine Potash Company was a venture between English investors and a Jewish director, a Mr. Novomeysky. He was a Siberian mining engineer who saw the Dead Sea and fell in love with it. In contrast to the British, he recognized the potential in its water. Novomeysky gath-

At the Palestine Potash Company power plant
Gad Granach is on the far right

ered a number of fellow countrymen from Siberia to come
along with him. Siberian Jews are something else, not to
be judged by the usual standards. Whosoever survives Siberia, can survive anywhere. They were adventurous, great
fellows who spoke Russian and Chinese, and together with
Novomeysky, built the plant.

Before working as a locomotive driver, I shoveled salt
leach. With our shirts off and wearing thick rubber boots,
we worked like the devil shoveling hot brine. In the beginning we took extra care that the stuff didn't run down the
handle and get on our hands. By the end of the day our
hands were all red and torn up. The first night I laid in bed
holding my wounded hands in the air, they hurt so badly.
After a while though, I didn't feel a thing. Man indeed gets
used to anything.

At the camp

We always watched how the Arab workers did the job. They were Bedouins from the surrounding area and their threshold for pain was considerably higher than ours. They stood barefoot in the salt leach the entire time and would laugh at us in our rubber boots. Then we understood what it meant to be "sons of the desert." We learned a great deal from the Bedouins. In those days we worked together and wouldn't have imagined that we'd be enemies one day, shooting at each other. It was striking, however, that the Bedouins didn't help one another. Each loaded up his own wagon, and when he was finished, just sat down and relaxed. For us it was different. When one of us was weaker we may have complained about him, but we'd help him load his wagon. We were used to doing things that way from the kibbutz.

In Kalya, on the northern end of the Dead Sea, a German Jew named Harry Levy built a hotel in the early years, the legendary Kalya Hotel. It was a top-class hotel with the maitre d'hôtel dressed in tails. They received their electricity from our northern factory at the Dead Sea. During the summer, there were so-called "moonlight trips" from Jerusalem to Kalya. You boarded a bus on Jaffa Street at 8pm and headed down to the Dead Sea to go dancing. The hotel had a platform extending out over the water and it gently rocked as we danced in the moonlight. It's indescribably beautiful when the moon shines over the Dead Sea at night and nearly as bright as daylight. When I had the night shift on the small locomotive, I could read the newspaper by the light of the moon.

Jews weren't the only guests that coming to the Kalya Hotel. Mostly there were wealthy Arabs from Jericho

By the Dead Sea

and British officers from Transjordan with their ladies. It was like a film set in British colonial India. At midnight the bus drove back to Jerusalem. David Ben Gurion, who later became Prime Minister, and his wife Paula were frequent guests at the hotel. Paula took excellent care of him. Without her nothing worked. Once at the hotel she called for a doctor. Ben Gurion wasn't feeling well and so the doctor came to examine him. She said, "It's not for me, it's not for him, it's for all of us because he's Ben Gurion and he's important for us." That was in 1945.

It was a wonderful time, that period when I drove the train along the Dead Sea. But what is a wonderful time really? There are brief moments in life which make all the

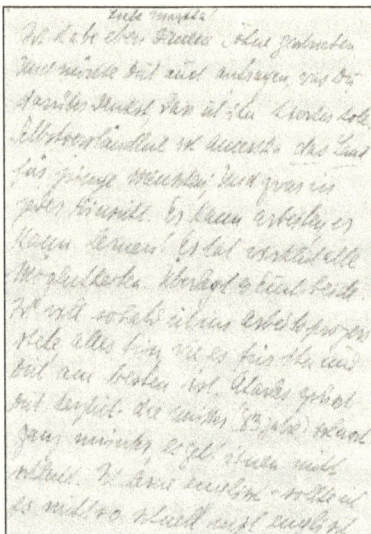

Letter from Alexander
Granach to Martha Granach

"Dear Martha, I've written your son and now want to ask you how you feel about bringing him here. America truly is the country for young people in every way. He could work, he could study, he'd really have every opportunity. Both of you should think it over. I might find him a job first before he comes and from then on do what's best for you and him. Charles sends you his best. Mother [83 years old] is lively and well and everyone else is doing fine."

effort seem worthwhile, yet they always go by so quickly. It is such a waste what we do with our lives.

I learned of the death of my father while I was down at the Dead Sea. I was in the cafeteria for breakfast where there were always lots of papers around such as *The Palestine Post* and *The Egyptian Mail*. Suddenly I see in print "Actor Alex G. Dies." Oddly his last name wasn't spelled out in full, but I knew immediately: that's my father. Everything else written about him was exactly right. No one in his family had bothered to tell my mother or I of his passing. Letters had been exchanged between us and in one of his last to my mother he asked if she would oppose my coming to America. Because of that, I had gotten myself a Palestinian passport. And suddenly, I read in the paper that he's gone.

I continued working for the Palestine Potash Company after leaving the kibbutz, and rented a room in Jerusalem. It was a special pleasure to be able to go there every two or three days from work at the Dead Sea. Each bus had its own *gabbai*, like in the synagogue, making sure that the workers always got their same seat on the bus. Workers are some of the most conservative beings in the world. It's just impossible to take one away from a machine on which, year in and year out, he's been pulling the same old lever. Give him something else to do, and he'll oppose it. His whole life he just wants to pull the same lever, and for his entire life he wants that one same seat on the bus.

I rented a furnished room in Jerusalem, in the home of

so-called "better people," in my case, with the Ginzburg family. The husband was the Editor in Chief of *Ha'aretz* newspaper. The household was a kosher one primarily because of the grandfather, an old-style Englishman who would go to the synagogue in summer dressed in a white suit. My room, however, was a safe haven where the rest of the Ginzburgs fled on Friday evening and Saturday to smoke. The grandfather wouldn't have allowed that on Shabbat under any circumstances. He was always making sure that everything was nice and kosher.

"From ten o'clock on, no lady visitors allowed" had been the rule in Germany, but not in Palestine. You could be very observant, but what you did in private was considered nobody else's business. Since I shared the room with another fellow, it cost me only two and a half Palestine pounds a month. I was making thirty-nine a month so I could have afforded a room all to myself, but the thought never really occurred to me. Everything had to be a little hard and uncomfortable, as after all, we were pioneers and busy building a new country. A room all to yourself just didn't seem to fit into that picture.

My roommate was Mr. Jabroff. He was around fifty and in my eyes then an old fart. He had a girlfriend though. He was a typical bachelor with quirky habits. For example, he collected toothbrushes for fear that one day there wouldn't be any left. And razor blades—he had a stockpile to last the next thirty years. When I asked if he could loan me one, he said no. We both worked shifts at the Dead Sea and had agreed that one of us would always be in town while the other was down at the Dead Sea so each could have the room to himself. That would have worked out fine, only he didn't keep his end of the bargain. I'd come home after the second shift at three in the afternoon looking forward to the evening, and there he was sitting on the bed. He'd grin and say in his rolling Russian accent, "I'm here too! I'm also off!" Oh wonderful, *mazel tov*. You can just imagine how excited I was about it. I had my own plans for the evening too, but what could you do? A trip to the movies was the only option.

Back then there was one movie house after another and they were always packed. On Saturday nights people had to stand in lines at the box office and tickets sometimes resold for double the price. Movies weren't being dubbed yet, of course, and subtitles hadn't come out yet either, but films were translated into three languages by inventive means. The translations ran on narrow rolls of paper going from top to bottom on both sides of the screen; one side had English or French, the other Hebrew and Arabic. You had your pick. They were handwritten on strips barely wide enough for a single word. Next to the screen sat students using both hands to wind the strips along with the film. Unfortunately, by the second showing it often happened that a winder fell asleep during the show. The film kept running but the translation stopped. Somebody in the audience would shout out "*Tirgum! Tirgum!*—Translation! Translation!" The poor student would hastily start winding again, but with too much force sending the reels spinning out of control. Now you couldn't read anything at all. So the film and the translation had to be rolled back and shown again for the audience not to miss anything. It could often be a really trying experience.

If you chose to go to the second showing, the ground beneath your feet would be carpeted in sunflower seed shells. Smoking was permitted and there were little tables to set your beer on. Eventually someone would set an empty bottle to rolling down the aisle, making it impossible to concentrate on the film. You were listening, watching, waiting for it to come to a full stop at the bottom of the hall. If, God forbid, the thing stopped somewhere in the middle, someone would always nudge it on again until it reached the bottom. By that time you were completely irritated and jittery.

Jerusalem was quite a wild place during the Mandatory period. It was a vibrant capital in the Middle East, a truly cosmopolitan city with a cosmopolitan past. For thousands of years the ancients had passed through here: Romans, Greeks, Persians, Babylonians, Arabs, Turks, and Crusaders. There were parties, evening dances, chamber concerts and performances—no comparison with what Jerusalem is like today. The *yekkes* brought a lot of this cosmopolitan atmosphere to Jerusalem, trying to pick up where they had left off in Germany. During the British Mandate, the city was also filled with spies. I remember a German Count von Hardenberg, an interesting character who snuck away from the Nazis to Turkey and then went over to the British, who in turn shipped him off to Palestine where a Jewish widow looked after him. He even got the suits belonging to her late husband. Later, the Grand Mufti of Jerusalem had him murdered in Beirut. The King of Ethiopia, "the Negus of Abyssinia" was living at the King David Hotel, the High Commissioner was in Jerusalem, and golf was played. It was a virtual parade of who's who and nobody would have dreamed of closing a coffeehouse early on Friday nights. Jerusalem was alive all through the night. It was wartime, there were blackouts, but the bars were busting at the seams with people. We were dancing on the volcano, and we knew it.

Tel Aviv, by comparison, was insignificant back then, just a small town in the sand. There's was a joke about three women from Tel Aviv strolling along the beach in the 1940s. They see a naked man lying in the sun with a newspaper over his head. The first woman says to the second, "Look, isn't that your husband over there?" The third one says, "No, that's not her husband." The second one then adds, "He's not even from Tel Aviv."

Jerusalem was politically and culturally central during the Mandatory period. Already in 1924, the Hebrew University had been established. The professors lived here in Jerusalem, the British administrative authority was located here, and the renowned Bezalel Art School. The German Jews founded Rehavia here too, and it's still the neighborhood with the most trees. The intellectual level in Jerusalem was uncommonly high. Naturally there were a few crazy people among them as well. One particularly eccentric character was the poet Else Lasker-Schueler. I recall how she would occasionally stop by to see my mother, who always saved newspapers for her. A circle of various people looked after her. Else Lasker-Schueler could only sleep in a lounge chair. Once they bought her a bed, which then she never used of course. She just continued sleeping in the chair. She went around Jerusalem wearing a fur coat, even in summer, and the children threw stones after her. In the Middle East, anything that comes across as strange of foreign is met with stone throwing—if it's moving, that is. Children here seem to be born with a natural tendency to throw stones. And I don't just mean the Arab children by the way, but Jewish ones as well. The Middle East apparently has some intrinsic connection with stone throwing. Maybe it's because there are so many of them here. A child has barely crawled out of its mother and already it's busy looking for a stone to throw.

Jerusalem's Ben-Yehuda Street was full of cafés, and in each one a particular group of people would gather. The Hungarians had their spot, the *yekkes* had theirs, and the Polish Jews went someplace else. Where you could smell the food, that's where the Hungarians were. There were always newspapers in the cafés, and you could sit with a cup of coffee reading for four, five hours. They had nice large newspaper and magazine racks with at least ten different subscriptions, just like the "Lesezirkel" or reading circle in Germany. The *yekkes* introduced that here. It was indeed wartime, but newspapers from everywhere made it here: the *Zürcher Zeitung*, the *Zürcher Illustrierte*, amd the *Schweizer Illustrierte*, they even came from Germany. The British papers were especially sought after to read the latest about the Royals, which was always on the front page.

In 1938 the famous Café Atara opened in Jerusalem. Whenever I came back from the Dead Sea, I would head straight there, that was our meeting spot. The "Atara" was a copy of the famous "Zuntz sel. Witwe" coffeehouse in Berlin, with everything done in brown tones utilizing a coffee bean motif. The waitresses wore little white aprons with a pocket in the front. They had an array of cakes to choose from. There was an Atara in Haifa and another in Tel Aviv. The café belonged to the Perlmutter Family. Mrs. Perlmutter always counted the napkins, typical Israeli napkins the standard size of which is about that of a postage stamp. You can't even blow your nose with one and if you try, it just goes straight through. The *yekkes* went to Atara for tea and would squabble over magazines if anyone tried to hoard the entire pile to himself. The Atara was Europe.

Café Alaska distinguished itself from the others chiefly by their cute waitresses, most of them new immigrants from Germany. I remember one in particular, very elegant with long legs. I always wanted to invite her to the movies, but it never happened. The Sichel Café had a large garden area in the back and a real mix of patrons. This one Sephardic Jews frequented as well. On the corner of Ben-Yehuda Street and Jaffa Street was the Café Vienna which had various newspapers in English like *The Palestine Post* and *The Egyptian Mail*. Wealthy Arabs came and read these. Across the street was the Europa Café where afternoon dances were held. Here the British officers went with their ladies. It was for officers only—off limits to regular soldiers. Well-to-do Jews and Arabs also went there. The Europa was a very fine café and it was considered bad form to be heard speaking any language other than English. The waiters wore black suits and bow ties. All along the walls were frescos by the artist Jacob Steinhardt, one of our greatest painters. Each fresco portrayed a different city in Palestine. Artists earned a living through such commissions, since not many people were buying paintings at the time. When the Europa was renovated, nobody thought of rescuing those frescoes.

Fink's Bar wasn't for everyone, but it was a very "in" place. All the top journalists gathered at Fink's. The young Churchill also frequented it. Everyone who wanted to find out what was really going on went to Fink's. One block further, near where Café Rimon is today and up on the third floor, was the Savyon, a fantastic nightclub decorated in red. It might have looked like a very upscale brothel, but it was, in fact, an elegant establishment into which regular people did not dare enter, thankfully. Substantial class differences still existed back then. For example, I never went to the King David Hotel during the Mandatory period because I clearly knew that it wasn't my place to be there. Today, however, everyone goes everywhere, and any normal shmuck can sit in the Breakfast Room of the King David, feeling he has arrived. And that's just how it looks.

Katty-corner from the King David was the Vienna Tea Room run by *yekkes*. The waitresses were beautiful German-Jewish girls who had left the kibbutz. At the Vienna sat well-to-do Brits drinking tea from small warmed tea pots, where the milk was always poured first into the cups to avoid tea stains from forming in them. The cakes they served there were marvelous and everyone spoke in German or English.

Jaffa Street, Jerusalem, during the Mandate period

The very nicest cafés of all, I will say, were outside of Jerusalem, in Nahariya, all of them securely in German-Jewish hands. The Penguin Café still exists there today. You went to Nahariya for strawberries with whipped cream, practically impossible to get anywhere else. It was the *yekkes* who first introduced sweet whipped cream here. Before that there was only a kind of sour cream that the Poles were used to having, but at the Penguin, you could have your fill of the good stuff. Strauss, a German business that started off in Nahariya with a single cow, was the first to make sweet whipped cream here. Today Strauss has operations all over the world. It all began with just one single cow they had. They milked it, sold the milk, and made cheese. Strauss produced exactly the kinds of things the *yekkes* liked to eat. Tnuva was Strauss's Polish competition. It was a dairy cooperative located on the kibbutz, yet of very high quality. When I first arrived in 1936, they were already packaging their butter in silver paper. But they showed no interest whatsoever in producing whipped cream.

You could also find strawberries and whipped cream in the German Colony of the Templars in Jerusalem, which existed up until 1941. The Templars, Protestant settlers from Swabia, Germany, came to Palestine at the end of the 19th century. Things with them were so German, that even their Arab workers spoke in Swabian dialect. The British and the German Jews used to go there. On Shabbat one went there to eat *schweinebraten* (roasted pork, very unkosher) and drink beer.

In Tel Aviv's German Colony was the Wagner factory. In 1938 the factory owner become involved in some affairs with the Nazis and was shot by the Jewish underground organization *Haganah*. The most famous German Colony though was located in Haifa, which even had a memorial to Kaiser Wilhelm II. In Jaffa a German consul resided up until 1941 and a flag with a swastika waved. The Templar children were all in the Hitler Youth, yet otherwise lived with their Jewish neighbors in peace. In 1941 they were interned by the British and sent to Australia as enemy aliens.

Back in Jerusalem, the *yekkes* also opened delicatessens on Ben-Yehuda Street and on Jaffa Road. One was named Sternschuss, there was also Levy, and Futter as well. None of these were kosher. Only German was spoken at Futter's Delicatessen, and everything was very refined. Herr Futter was rather cold, but Frau Futter was a real beauty. How the two got together I'll never know. They had wonderful ham though, very thinly sliced, and they addressed every customer by name. The ham probably came from Nazareth where the Christian Arabs raised pigs.

Doing business with Arabs went splendidly. If, however, you lived in Rehavia, you had little contact with Arabs. An exception was with certain people in well-to-do circles who liked to make mention of their cultivated Arab friends. It's still like that today. People tried to show how cosmopolitan they were and used very sophisticated language. The *yekkes* of course maintained their penchant for evening chamber music performances during which you could hardly whisper a word. It was excruciatingly boring.

When World War II broke out, suddenly no one was speaking German anymore. In 1938 German—and even Yiddish—were held in such disregard that fanatics from the Histadrut labor union threw a hand grenade into the offices of a German language newspaper *Blumenfelds Neueste Nachrichten*. You were now supposed to forget, as quickly as possible, every bit of culture you had brought over with you. Nevertheless, the majority of *yekkes* hadn't learned Hebrew properly, and when they had, they were so perfectionist and exacting about it. That was awful too. They only had to say *"Shalom"* and already it came out sounding like *"Deutschland, Deutschland über alles!"*

A few former actors, working at all kinds of odd jobs then, had opened a German theater club. They performed German classics while offering coffee and cake. Later, they had to rent smaller spaces in secret and performed underground German theater. One of them organized a theatrical group called *die Bruecke* ("The Bridge"). His wife was a waitress at the Atara Café and he was a window display decorator, but his true passion was the theater. In one of their performance I heard the line "What is that I see...Prussian uniforms?" and then two men appeared in just plain clothes. They simply couldn't get ahold of any uniforms. With very limited resources and lots of enthusiasm, underground German theater was performed in the middle of the war. All the *yekkes* from Rehavia were finally able to see some German theater again.

At some point, the German General Rommel was fifty miles from Cairo, and we started to become rather anxious. Jews pressed the British hard to do something. Many wanted to volunteer for the army, but the British weren't keen on the offer. Eventually, they said they would allow us to create a "Jewish Brigade," but only under the condition that Arabs too, in equal numbers, would volunteer for an Arab unit. Of course this was completely absurd as the Arabs had no particular reason to fight against Hitler. To the contrary, if anything, they were sympathizers with the Germans in the fight against the British. Some Arabs still become stary-eyed and rave from Hitler when they meet Germans today

Ultimately, the Jewish Brigade was founded under the command of a certain Mr. Benjamin from Australia. This was intended to be the foundation stone of what would later become the Israeli army. In 1941 Tel Aviv was bombed. I was at Kibbutz Shfayim at the time, nine miles away. We heard the bombs and ran into our trenches. I still remember vividly how frightened we were, awaiting a major attack. All that came were three dinky Italian planes from Sicily, but in Tel Aviv there were over 150 casualities.

More and more reports reached us about the extermination of Jews. A few of those who managed to escape the concentration camps told of what was going on in Europe. To think about the Holocaust now and try to imagine what was happening on any given day in 1943, over here and back there, my God! What was I doing on that day? I was sitting around by the Dead Sea, eating a wonderful meal, and debating who I was going to sleep with or other such banalities. I was shooing flies away, or getting the sand out from between my toes. Everyone who was living here then has a guilty conscience; they'll never be free of that, whether they like it or not.

But what were the American Jews doing at the time? In the US, there were millions of Jews then, and here barely 600,000, hardly anything. Don't the American Jews have a guilty conscience? In contrast to us in Israel, they didn't want to know what was going on and were even upset when Jews from Germany started arriving in 1933, treating them like undesirables. Talk about "Jewish solidarity!" In America, such Jewish solidarity didn't take hold until after the war was over. One showed solidarity with the dead. They took no timely action in response to events in Europe, behaving as if they just didn't want to cause a stir. Why not bomb Auschwitz? Why not negotiate with the Nazis? Here in Israel, Rudolph Kastner[s] negotiated with the Nazis and saved a couple hundred lives. For this fanatics shot him in Tel Aviv. Because of their own guilty conscience, they shot him.

When World War II came to an end, the war here really got started. More and more violence erupted between Arabs and Jews. As a result, the United Nations decided in 1947 to partition Palestine into Jewish and Arab regions. The Jews accepted the partition plan, but the Arabs did not.

Our trips to the Dead Sea became increasingly dicey, with Arabs shooting at us along the road to Jericho. We could only travel to there in convoys with protection from the British. Any other way would have been too dangerous. The Arabs insisted that the windows of our buses be covered so we couldn't see out. They set up all these conditions, and we were always trying to meet them just to avoid getting them upset. Apropos getting upset; one fellow asks the other, "After 25 years of marriage, what is it about your wife that can still upset you? They guy answers, "Every word!"

That's how it was between the Arabs and the Jews. There we sat in 98° heat in a quasi-armored bus without windows, going nuts with fear. What guarantee was there that in the event of an Arab attack, the British wouldn't just bail out and leave us behind sitting on the bus? Such things certainly happened. Once for example, they arrested a couple of Jews who belonged to an underground organization and tossed them out of a car at Jaffa Gate, of all places. They could have been torn to pieces on the spot by Arabs. We could never rely on the British.

With these convoys we transported not only potash to Jerusalem but also supplies of weapons. The weapons came by air from Czechoslovakia to the Dead Sea where we loaded them onto trucks with secret compartments beneath the floorboards. I unloaded them myself. There were heavy machine guns with swastikas still on them. Our shadow government, Golda Meir, and the other Zionist leaders were also able to make it to Jerusalem with the help of these convoys, having first been flown to the Dead Sea from Tel Aviv. The road from Tel Aviv to Jerusalem was blocked off.

On March 23rd, 1948 I went with a convoy from Jerusalem to the Dead Sea for the last time. From then on, the British wouldn't guarantee our safety any longer. They'd had enough of us and were pulling out.

There are politicians who say that the British abandoned Palestine due to Jewish resistance. That, however, is nothing but a myth. The British abandoned this country for economic reasons, just as they had done in India. The country wasn't yielding anything and had become absolutely unimportant for them. Not a single Jew or Arab ever paid one cent of tax to the British treasury. Bribery was rampant here. Everything was greased with payoffs; practically any British official could be had for a price. WWII was over and they no longer needed passage through the Suez Canal... so now they could simply pull out. The British Empire was bankrupt so what did it still want with Palestine? To hang around and fight with Jews and Arabs? In court the presiding judge was always a Briton, flanked by a Jewish judge and an Arab judge. The Jewish judge convicted the Arabs and the Arab judge convicted the Jews and the British judge sat happily in the middle. Basically they had nothing but trouble here.

Even today, there are those who still believe that our underground organizations forced the British to leave the country. Right, sure. The British sold this land, just like they sold tanks, military camps, and provisions. Sometimes even twice. For example, we purchased the Schneller school compound in Jerusalem from the British, even though they had already sold it to the Arabs.

The British left this country quite ingloriously, like thieves in the night. And when they did, everything fell apart behind them. That's just what they wanted. The Arab Legion, which had been commimisioned and financed by the British, stood ready in the Old City, and it wouldn't have displeased the British very much to see them conquer us. During WWII, Jews went to the front, fought and died, and then the Arabs marched in the victory parade with us. They looked so much more picturesque than we did, with their horses and camels. The Jewish Brigade fought in Italy during the war, yet the Arabs took part in the victory parade in London. The world is filled with contradictions and injustices.

The British slipped out of Palestine, handing nothing over legally, just leaving everything behind. When they left, part of Jerusalem was occupied by Arab Legion soldiers. The whole Russian Compound in the middle of the Jewish part of the city was in the hands of the Arabs. For our defense we just had the Jewish underground organizations *Haganah*, *Etzel,* and *Lechi*, and practically no weapons. The British tried their best to disarm the Jews in Palestine and they almost succeeded. From 1946 on, they had nothing better to do than to search for illegal Jewish weapons. Unfortunately, they did a good job. I was at the Dead Sea watching when a British officer took his bamboo swagger stick, pointed at a certain spot on the ground and said, "Dig here." They found rifles, machine guns, and grenades. It was hard to watch. Later they searched the power station and my Parker fountain pen too became a war casualty. A few British officers sympathized with the Jews, but most were on the side of the Arabs and would have been glad to see them win.

On the 14th of May 1948, the British left Palestine and on the same day the State of Israel was declared. At the time I was at the northern end of the Dead Sea. On May 13th we still would have cockily said, we can defend ourselves against the Arabs, but on May 15th we fled as fast as we could leaving it all behind. We had no other choice with an Arab Legion located right next-door in Jericho. We loaded up all the boats and headed south. The *kibbutzniks* even left their cows behind, taking only chickens with them. They would have been better off doing the opposite. I didn't leave the Dead Sea area until 1949. When I came back to Tel Aviv, I saw Jewish policemen for the first time in the old British uniforms, I understood then that the State of Israel had been born. From now on we would have to behave like any other normal people and get used to being kicked around by our own policemen, including getting traffic tickets and such. That's what states are for.

B en Gurion had barely declared Israel's statehood
when six Arab armies began their invasions. They were
coming in from every corner: from Egypt, Jordan, Syria,
Iraq and Lebanon, even the Saudis were represented with
a contingent. Each tried to snatch for itself whatever there
was to be had. The United Nations merely imposed a new
embargo, sticking to their usual practice of not taking sides
under any circumstances, least of all with the Jews! We,
however, had already accepted the UN partition plan. We
would have received the smaller part of the partition and
all of Galilee would have gone to the Arabs. But, instead of
recognizing the plan for partition and having their state,
Glubb Pasha and his Arab Legion started bombing Jerusalem.

Half of Ben-Yehuda Street was blown to bits in 1948.
The Jewish quarters of the Old City were defended for six
weeks and when the big heroes of the Arab Legion were
finally able to capture it, all they found were a mere thirty
Jewish fighters with rifles—no army, not even one canon.
That was an embarrassment for them. The Syrians were
poised to conquer Galilee, and the Egyptians were halfway
to Tel Aviv. They were at Kibbutz Ramat Rachel on the out-
skirts of Jerusalem, and nobody gave a damn, no country
was going to help us. The Iraqis were at Kibbutz Ramat

Hakovesh, north of Tel Aviv, and that little kibbutz held off an entire Iraqi division. I still ask myself, what on earth did they want here? At some point, however, the war turned in our favor. First we encircled the Egyptians, with a young officer among them named Abd al-Nasser, and then we took the Negev and Eilat where the Jordanians were. Finally, when the Druze who lived in Palestine joined us, we were able to bring the Syrians to a standstill. The Druze were excellent fighters.

The Israelis forced back all of the Arab armies and in the process even conquered areas that, according to the partition plan, would have belonged to the Arabs. And then, suddenly, the world claims that we should return it all. It was as if we were the ones who began the attack, rather than fighting a defensive war. Six thousand Jews died in 1948. Was that for nothing? That's not how things work. It's like a neighbor who throws a rock through your window and then demands the rock back.

Fortunately, we learned more in the *Haganah* than just standing at attention and parade marching. We had training in close contact fighting, jiu-jitsu, and the use of hand grenades. That was a real dangerous affair; they were the kind you had to light with a match. Such a device you want to rid yourself of as fast possible.

When I was drafted in 1948 and sent to the Dead Sea there wasn't any heavy fighting. Our local military commander got ambitious once, thinking we should attack the Arab village on the other side. That was a mistake. We had been stationed peacefully by the Sea when the Arabs cut off our water supply forcing us to drink water from a spring that was filled with salt. You can get used to it, though I couldn't drink normal water for a while afterwards; it seemed to have no taste. In the other village across the Sea were Circassians, an elite Arab unit. The bodyguards of King Hussein were Circassians. So our meshuggener commander got bored and decided to attack the village. We had fifty *Palmach* men and fifty regular men, all with zero war experience and poorly armed. Of course it was a major disaster. The next day they fired upon us with British artillery from the Jordanian side. We couldn't run away as fast as they fired at us. We retreated into the Dead Sea Caves where we were safe until the bombardment ended. That was our contribution to the War of Independence.

Up until 1948, we Jews were called Palestinians, while the Arabs called themselves Arabs. Maybe they got the idea of calling themselves Palestinians from us. Many Arabs here were also not from Palestine. They came from everywhere: from Egypt, Transjordan, and Syria, since the land did at one time belong to Greater Syria. In Jerusalem today the Father Schneller school building is still standing, with the inscription: "Schneller's Syrian Orphanage—The Lord blesses our coming and the Lord blesses our leaving." The Syrian dream was and still is, to possess everything here. If I were an Arab, I too would want to conquer Tel Aviv. Nevertheless, Syria was only a Turkish province that was split off in 1918-1919, and Transjordan too was a British creation—it hadn't existed before. Iraq was a province as well. And when Arabs today say that Israel is an artificial construction, they should simmer down and look at history, because most of their countries are artificial constructions too! Absolutely everything here belonged to the Ottoman Empire previously, and all the other ruling powers tried to take as much as they could here. Jesus and the first Christians were not Palestinians even if that is what Palestinian politician Hanan Ashrawi has told the whole world. Jesus and the first Christians were Jews, but this is not something Ashrawi mentions. If you like, then I am a Palestinian. I swore allegiance to the Palestinian state in November 1945. My Palestine passport is still in my closet.

Government of Palestine.

PALESTINIAN CITIZENSHIP ORDERS, 1925-42. ,1925

CERTIFICATE OF NATURALIZATION.

Whereas Gerhard GRANACH

(hereinafter called the "applicant") has applied for a Certificate of Naturalization, alleging with respect to himself (herself) the particulars set out below, and has satisfied me that the conditions laid down in the above mentioned Orders for the grant of a Certificate of Naturalization are fulfilled in his (her) case:

Now, therefore, in pursuance of the powers conferred on me by the said Orders,

I grant to the said applicant this Certificate of Naturalization and declare that he (she) shall, subject to the provisions of the said Orders, be entitled to all political and other rights, powers and privileges, and be subject to all obligations, duties and liabilities to which a natural-born Palestinian citizen is entitled or subject, and have to all intents and purposes the status of a natural-born Palestinian citizen.

In witness whereof I have hereto subscribed my name

this   **twelfth**   day of   **November** .

JERUSALEM ירושלים القدس

68678   A   Serial Number of Application   891

Palestine certificate of naturalization, November 1945

After the founding of the State of Israel, the wild days here were over and done with. Jerusalem became a little Jewish *shtetl* filled with Jewish petite bourgeoisie. Most of the foreigners were suddenly gone, and what did we get instead? Pious American Jews with their *kippas*. Jerusalem went to sleep and became a provincial town, and the pious types came slowly creeping out of the woodwork. There's a little anecdote related to this, about the British officer who comes to visit Jerusalem after the war and stays at the King David Hotel. On a Friday evening at 9:00 pm, he steps out of the hotel, looks left, looks right, and says, "Oh dear God... do they still have a curfew here?"

Since the presence of observant Jews began to grow here, Jerusalem became like a ghost town on Shabbat. Before, they were hardly to be seen. They only came out from their self-made ghetto on Friday afternoons to run around Jaffa Street shouting, "*Shabbes, Shabbes!*" They wanted Jewish businesses to close shop for the Sabbath, but people just laughed them off. Jerusalem had been a garrison town with an international flair, where not only Jews had lived, but Britons, French, Greek military, and any and all of those who had fled the Nazis. But all of that changed after 1948.

My mother worked in Palestine as a housekeeper and in the beginning helped raise the children of a wealthy family from Haifa in the spirit of Rosa Luxemburg. She lived there like a member of the family. She cooked and washed and looked after everything. One day, however, when the lady of the house thought mother could take a bath in her used bath water, she decided it was time to move. Then she was with another family in Jerusalem until her retirement. Mother really enjoyed her autumn years. She read a great deal and went with her lady friends to see German plays.

She was too old to learn Hebrew. Hebrew was the language of the younger generation. There's an anecdote about that, how in Nahariya, founded by German Jews, one *yekke* starts to address another in Hebrew, *"Shalom, Adon Kohn, ma shlomcha?*–Good day Mr. Kohn, how are you doing?" Then the other one says in German, "Oh come on, speak German, will you please? We're not kids!"

My mother lived thirty-three years in total in Palestine and Israel but despite this she hardly knew any Hebrew, and what she did know she tended to mispronounce. She moved inot a retirement home when she turned eighty. Whenever I came to visit, she made sure that everyone knew and understood that I was her son. Even without Hebrew, my mother did an exceedingly good job of making herself understood by simply speaking German with everyone, and indeed very loudly so one could understand her well.

She was the absolute stereotypical *yekke*. There was a phrase she would say, one that accompanied her over her entire life. It was, you might say, like the national hymn of all the German Jews: "Das ist mir sehr peinlich!–Oh how embarrassing that is!" She had her bank account at the Feuchtwanger Bank, where naturally German was spoken. Every time she dropped in to pick up her social security check, she would say to the teller, somewhat embarrassed, "Yes, here I am again." And at the end she would thank the

Martha Granach, Jerusalem 1958

teller as if she had personally given my mother the money out of her own pocket.

Pious religious folks always really got on her nerves, especially much later at the retirement home where the religious services held no interest for her. At the home was a certain Herr Marx, for whom which she had eyes. She'd hook herself onto his arm and they'd go for walks together. There was another woman in the home that had eyes for Herr Marx too, though not for taking walks but for studying Talmud together. Frau Winter came from a observant background and was the mother-in-law of a well known philosopher, Yeshayahu Leibowitz. Whenever Frau Winter pulled Herr Marx away from my mother again, she'd get upset over the two sticking their noses in those pious books saying, "Oh such scatterbrained nonsense. Big self important to-do. What they really need is some fresh air!"

Although she never learned Hebrew, she did learn Yiddish. On *Kol Yisrael*, the Voice of Israel, which was the only radio station around then, was Yiddish news every evening at seven read by mother's darling, Reuven Rubinstein. That hour was so sacred to her that all ready at a quarter to seven you couldn't talk to her. Ten minutes to seven at the latest, she'd nervously start tuning in on the radio to make sure that, God forbid, Reuven Rubinstein didn't start talking without her there to hear it.

This news program was as strange as it was provincial. It often went something like this: *A giten Obend ind a giten Schabbes, meine lieben Zuherer ind Zuhererinnen. Hert jetzt die Jedijes, gelesint von Reuven Rubinstein: Arabische Merder hoben sich heriebergerangelt iber den*

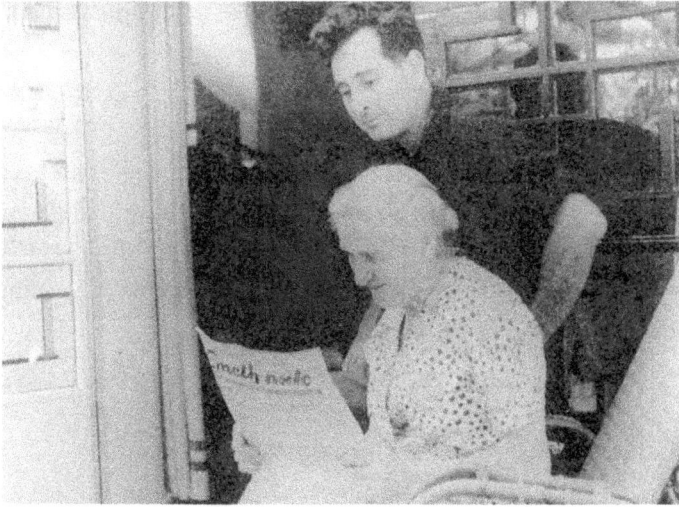

With mother in Jerusalem

Grenze, man hot geschossen mit Gewehren, ind man hot geschossen auf jiddische Landarbeiter. Ober jiddische Blut wird nicht umsonst vergossen! Jiddische Seldner hoben sich nicht derschrocken. Men hot se ausgeschochten ind geschluggen, die Feinde von Israel. Schabbat Schalom! (Roughly: "A good evening and a good Shabbat to our listeners. Here's Reuven Rubenstein with the day's news: Armed Arab murderers crossed the border and fired shots at Jewish field workers. Jewish blood, however, does not flow without consequence! The response was brave and the enemies of Israel were beaten back. Shabbat Shalom!") And about an earthquake somewhere it went: *Gewaltige Massen hoben sich arobgeworfen auf die Heiserlach ind hot sie zerkwetscht ind zerdrikt. Etlaeche Menschen sin-*

nen im gekommen ind gestorben. Groisse Tragedies und
Zores. Schabbat Schalom! ("Huge masses of earth tore
apart and tumbled upon small homes, taking many victims
inside to their death. An awful, terrible tragedy. Shabbat
Shalom!") In Yiddish, even the worst catastrophes sound-
ed only half as bad. I said to my mother once, "Here you
sit, in Israel, listening to the radio news in Yiddish. Now if
somebody had told you that was going to happen fifty years
ago in Berlin ..." She just laughed.

In 1956 I took over the technical organization of the
children's village Kiryat Yearim, not far from Jerusalem. It
was an institution of the *Jugend-Alijah,* "Youth Immigration," financed through donations from Switzerland. It was
a village for war orphans and other children. Often one did
not even know where they came from. In the beginning,
some children came from the Nazi concentration camps,
and later from different countries in the Middle East, then
wherever the latest wave of immigration came from. Most
of the children were quite traumatized and disturbed; some
screamed, others were silent. One boy had been found in
the Hamburg harbor with a sign hung around his neck on
which was written simply his name, *Selig* ("blessed" in
German)

I learned a great deal in Kiryat Yearim and don't regret
a single second that I spent there. Once you've lived and
worked with traumatized individuals, then you can get
along just fine with all the so-called "normal people" too.
The difference, by the way, isn't all that great.

Hebrew Union College opened in 1963. It was a large

Biblical archaeological center and reform Jewish seminary. I became acquainted with the director, Professor
Nelson Glueck. It was a kind of love at first sight. Glueck
was looking for a technical assistant and asked me if I knew
anyone. I said, "Of course I do, somebody I'm very close
to." "Who then?" he asked. "Me" I said. "Great" he said,
and so I moved to Jerusalem and became the Superinten-
dent for Buildings and Grounds. They built a complex that
housed a school, a synagogue, a seminary, and a library
with an emphasis on biblical archaeology. Hebrew Union
College was a fantastic workplace. We received large con-
tributions from America for excavations. Every summer

American students and their instructors would come over, as well as various volunteers, from pastors out of Nevada to nuns from Brazil. All were decked out from head to toe with pith helmets, knives, ropes, compasses, and I can't even begin to talk about all the camera gear. They seemed to think they had arrived somewhere in the untamed wilderness. Once one of them came up to me and said in a loud voice, very slowly, and using exaggerated gestures with his hands so even a "native" idiot like me would understand "You tell cook... food good." I answered him, "Tomorrow sunrise on the hill. White man will die." He got the message.

There were a good number of Germans on the expeditions as well. One of them was named Schmidt. What a character he was. I'd always annoy him during our excavations. From behind him I'd roar, "SCHMIDT!!!" He'd jump up, all startled, and then I would say *"Weitermachen!"*— "Carry on!" Later in America, he became a reform Jew, but that wasn't enough for him. When he returned to Israel he became Orthodox and gave himself the name *Shar Yeshuv*—"Gate of the People." He had a beard three feet long with side curls, many children, also with side curls, and his wife wore a headscarf. He became mercilessly orthodox and every second sentence from him is now *"Baruch Hashem, Baruch Hashem"* (Bless the Lord). He lives in Haifa these days but could fit in really well with the Orthodox Jews in Mea Shearim. A few years ago, in Jerusalem's Old City, an allegedly Jewish cemetery was going to be excavated. The Orthodox Jews raised a fuss because one should not disturb the dead, and they cursed the director of the exca-

Excavations in Tel Gezer

With Inge at a Purim party

vation, a much admired Israeli scientist. Shortly after that, this great strong specimen of a man, suddenly collapsed. Heart attack, dead, at fifty. And what did the Orthodox do? They had a celebration because their prayers had been answered. What more do I have to say?

The religious Jews truly have a very personal relationship with God and they bother him whenever they can. He is responsible for everything that happens in daily life, absolutely everything. And when someone is lying on their deathbed, they hastily change his or her name to trick the Angel of Death who, apparently, requires a matching name and address for his services, like the postman. I believe we are basically only at the early stages of human civilization and that we have a very long way to go. But in case there is a God, I'd have one request for him: Make another group the chosen people, and leave us in peace. Take the Iraqis, or better yet, the Iranians. I'd gladly let them have the privilege.

I worked for Hebrew Union College seventeen years altogether, and during that time learned how to get things done smoothly without all that Middle Eastern fuss and chaos. Americans, with their equipment and organization, are hard to beat. On our expeditions we took along everything one could possibly think of, like a traveling circus in the middle of the desert. The only problem was that we didn't have Coca-Cola, and for Americans back then, nothing was complete without it. The Arab League was always quick to boycott, and Coca-Cola first chose not to sell in Israel out of fear of reprisal and loss of profits in the larger Arab market. Coke eventually started selling to Israel but Pepsi responded to the pressure of an Arab nation boycott and did not do business here. Pepsi became the cola consumed in Arab countries because Coca-Cola was served in Israel. Jews drank Coke and Arabs drank Pepsi. It would've been better had it been the other way around though. Then they wouldn't always have to say, "Bebsi blease." Arabs, you see, can't pronounce the letter "P."

In 1967 came the Six-Day War. The Egyptian president Nasser threw UN soldiers out of Gaza, blocked the Straits of Tiran,[1] and marched his whole army into the Sinai, and once again no other country protested. Maybe the UN Secretary-General, U Thant, thought Nasser just wanted to hold some folk dances in the Sinai, or maybe he thought Nasser closed off the Straits of Tiran just so the fish wouldn't swim through. Nasser cabled King Hussein of Jordan to say that he was already halfway to Tel Aviv and then Hussein decided to join the party. I'll never forget that day: At 10:45am on a Monday, Mr. Hussein had nothing better to do than to open fire on us, on Jerusalem, an open unarmed city, until six o' clock in the evening. Across from my house an entire family was wiped out. The next day he and his legion took over the former headquarters of the High Commissioner of Transjordan and Palestine and kicked out the UN stationed there. I watched as their convoys drove past Hebrew Union College.

In New York they didn't wake up to what was happening until the Israeli tanks had come in and taken everything back. When the Arabs occupied the UN headquarters, the prevailing sentiment was basically: Well that's war and these things happen in wars. However, when the Israelis re-conquered it: Return it immediately, it belongs to us! The UN was always blind in one eye, the one that looked in Israel's direction. Of course we did not give them the building back immediately. First we needed to sort through all those interesting papers lying around inside.

After that it went tit for tat: Monday and Tuesday the Jordanians bombarded West Jerusalem, but by Wednesday the tide had turned against them. On Thursday the Israelis conquered the Old City, and by Friday our head rabbi could blow his *shofar* there. And Nasser we drove into the Sinai, horse, rider and carriage. Euphoria reigned in Israel, and we thought of ourselves as "empire builders." The Palestinians, incidentally, didn't seem to be completely displeased with their new situation, as they had not been very happy under the Jordanians in West Jordan nor under the Egyptians in Gaza. They greeted the Israelis with white sheets, applause, and dancing. But what does that really mean? People always dance. They do it at soccer games in England and elsewhere, sometimes they're just like tons of extras playing "the masses" in a movie. But the Palestinians didn't rejoice for long.

When the Six-Day War was over the mood in Israel felt like a new awakening. Arabs from the Old City poured into *Mahane Yehuda*, the Jewish market in West Jerusalem, and bought *challah* and carp and other things that they didn't have. On Friday evening you could see them heading home with two *challahs* under each arm. And the Israelis too could go to East Jerusalem for the first time since 1948 and buy meat at "Siniora's" or *hummus* at "Abu Shukri"

once again. Only on Fridays around noon was it better not to be there, when Muslims came out of the mosque filled with fire and ready to battle the infidels of the world. They were always incited by their religious leaders against the Jews.

Back then there were still Arab shops and delicatessens in East Jerusalem. They looked like the ones in England. I used to buy Indian chutney there and Oxo cubes, the English equivalent to Maggi instant broth. One Oxo cube dissolved in a glass of hot water was an evening treat. In my view, Arabs and Jews can get along and live together when we buy from them and they from us.

Sometimes I wonder how things might have been if the Arabs, instead of reacting with xenophobia, had simply said "Welcome." We would have arrived as guests instead of conquerors and may have lived as good neighbors. I worked together with Arabs at the Dead Sea and we got along very well as co-workers and felt quite close to one another. Where is it written then, that dogs and cats must be at war? In my home, dogs and cats have lived together for years. There have always been Jews and Arabs in this land. Since the beginning of time people have been migrating here. The whole world undergoes migrations to this day. One group immigrates, the other runs away; always, somewhere, there are thousands fleeing. Like in the joke where two Jews in an airport pass each other on the escalator, one going up and the other down, one arriving, the other departing, and each calls out to the other, "Where are you going meshuggener?"

Yes, it's true that this land wasn't uninhabited when the Jews came, but neither was it overpopulated. To a great extent it belonged to Arab landowners who lived partly in Beirut or elsewhere, and were selling it off like wild to the Jewish National Fund. Many of the Arabs who actually farmed the land were tenant-farmers who worked under very harsh conditions. I must admit, we had no intention of helping them out of their plight, but we did build this country up and give it an infrastructure that didn't exist before. And with that we created jobs not only for us but for the Arabs too. It's often forgotten that some of the Arabs living here today came only after Jews had started immigrating to Palestine. There was indeed enough room here for both peoples to live together in peace.

Both sides have made many mistakes, and now the situation is extremely complicated. Enmity arises out of the fear that something will be taken away from you. If from the very beginning we had tried to explain to the Arabs that we didn't want to take anything away from them, and if they had tried to tell us that they did not want to chase us into the sea, if we had just communicated with one another, then everything here might have looked very different today.

After the Six-Day War, I ventured down to the Dead Sea to see the factory that we had to abandon overnight in 1948. I could not believe my eyes; there was nothing left of it! In addition to the potash plant, there had been living quarters, and now there was not one stone left standing. The Jordanians had destroyed everything. The ruins are still there today. All they had to do was walk into the plant, flip a switch, and everything would have worked just fine. Such a waste.

Hussein controlled the West Bank for nineteen years, but never built a single university during that time. He built nothing at all there even though the Arabs had substantially more money than the Israelis. Why do they spend it all on arms, actually? I don't want to paint a rosy picture, but Arab universities were first founded under Israeli occupation. Today though when there's "trouble" in them because students are demonstrating instead of studying, and the Israelis temporarily close the universities, this is reported all around the world. However, when the Israelis first opened the universities, news of this on television was nowhere to be seen. Before, when a Palestinian wanted to study he had to travel all the way to Cairo or Beruit. People forget about this too easily. They seem to believe the universities have been around since Suleiman the Magnificent.

Recently one of these pious Jewish settlers actually hit upon the idea that they should communicate better with their Arab neighbors instead of fighting against them. Apart from the fact that I have no clue why these lunatics have to live in the West Bank of all places, in the middle of all these Arabs who, understandably, do not want them there, the idea of communicating with one another I find fantastic— and a few years too late. They should have thought of this in 1967. Nevertheless, I am of the opinion that we should leave these so-called "settlers" out to dry, simply ignore them, neither supporting them nor protecting them. Let them fight the Arabs with their ludicrous guns that they're always carrying around with them. I have a gun at home too, but I'm not insane enough to run around with the thing. First of all, I don't need a sex symbol in my trouser pocket for my ego, and secondly, I don't have any ammunition for it. If the thing fires, it will only be with God's help. A Jewish saying goes: "If God wills it, then a broom may fire."

I am often asked how I can live under the constant threat here, yet I don't see it as such. When you live in New York, there are also certain streets you simply don't go down because they're life threatening. No white person can live in Harlem, but neither does he have to. It's the same situation here. Our settlers say, "Why shouldn't I be able to move to Nablus. It's still Israel isn't it?" No, you may not move to Nablus! One cannot live anywhere one wants. This is

With Schmuel Birger in Jerusalem's Old City after 1967

the case all over the world. The Bosnians cannot go where the Serbians are, and vice-versa. And no human being simply *must* live exactly in the place where he or she is not wanted.

The story of what would happen if we left the settlers in the West Bank alone by themselves would be a short one. They wouldn't make it through their first pogrom[2] there. What kind of "settlers" are they anyway? Have they done something for the land on which they "settle"? They haven't even planted a single shrub. Yesterday they were in Brooklyn, and today they want to tell me what Zionism is. In 1936 I settled on Arab land that was bought from the Arabs, and I actually worked and built upon the land. *Avodah Yehudi*, Jewish work, was really the thing back then. Arabs didn't build our houses back in those days which seems to be the norm now. There's a story about an Israeli walking down the street with his son on Shabbat: He says, "And do you see that house over there? I built it. And that street, I paved it when I was young. And there, the water pipes, I helped lay them down as well." The young son looks at him amazed and asks his father, "When you were young Dad, were you an Arab?"

I cannot understand why it never occurred to the Palestinians to say, "We are not going to build any houses for Israelis on the West Bank. Let them build their own damn houses by themselves!" If the Arabs had organized, a boycott like this would have worked, and there was money to support it. The Saudis invested millions of dollars in PLO terrorists and arms for years, and the money never ran out. But the Arabs never seemed able to unite among themselves, one village quarrels with the next one. They themselves have been the Israeli secret weapon number one.

Incidentally, there are few punks in Israel, basically none. People who stick clothespins through their cheeks are just the thing we're missing here. Nobody feels the need for that when we've seen enough real trouble in over fifty years of fighting. When I see how riots burst out at soccer games in Britain, I have to quote a friend who said, "What those folks are missing is war." That's how it is, unfortunately, when people feel they need to riot and rage. The Israelis have but one passion, driving, and they do indeed drive their cars like madmen. I think we have the highest accident rate in the world. If the Saudis would just buy each and every Israeli a fast sports car, they'd be rid of us in a year.

Arab society is unbelievably inhibited and therefore the modern Israelis must be like a thorn in their side, an eternal foreign body. Alone how they treat women—as long as he rides atop the donkey and she follows on foot with a basket on her head collecting wood, they remain a long way from democracy. To the Arabs, democracy is like putting a saddle on a cow. Their hate towards Israelis arises from a mixture of envy and admiration: We live in a free and open society, and our women do not run around under a veil. Israeli men can flirt with women anytime, and visa-versa. Arab men have to go to Hamburg when they want to be with a woman. That has to bring down a society when millions of men don't have sex! Arab envy is primarily penis envy. They should finally try to straighten things out within themselves, instead of believing that nothing will ever be right until they drive us out of here first.

Sometimes I wonder how things would be if the Israelis disappeared overnight—if the Arabs woke up one morning to find Israel gone. What then? Would they be happy? No they wouldn't be! They would have to find a new enemy right away, perhaps the entire Western culture. The real enemy isn't really us. Their true enemy is themselves and religious fundamentalism. There are two things that rule the world: sex and religion, and the problem is that the two do not mix together well.

I would really love to know why people become religious. It's especially difficult for me after Auschwitz. Maybe there is some kind of supernatural power, but nevertheless, what happens is all up to mankind, we are responsible. If I go

With dachshund "Pamela" around 1968

Jerusalem in the 1960's

through the forest and step on an anthill upsetting things, that doesn't make me the god of the ants. I'm just somebody who happened to walk by and destroy something. And for us when bad things happen, it isn't some extraterrestrial power that's to blame, but us alone. We shouldn't busy ourselves so much with God, but instead with humans, and above all we should be good to each other. But very few people can actually do this, and our own Orthodox seem particularly incapable of doing it.

Mea Shearim, the Orthodox Jews' quarter, I find awful. Nor do I ever go there. I do not see the romanticized picture that others see in this place. I see only backwardness, narrow-mindedness, and the shmutz. They're still living in the Middle Ages in every respect. Among Orthodox Jews, one marries at age seventeen or eighteen in order to bring as many children into the world as possible. That the "facts of life" are never explained to them and that they're not given the full lowdown goes without saying. Like the joke where on the morning after her honeymoon the *mame* asks the bride, "So! How was it? The bridegroom knew how to handle himself didn't he? He knew what to do, right?" The newlywed yells back, "*Mame*, he's a meshuggener!" The *mame* asks, "How's he a meshuggener?" The newlywed says, "Because he crawls on top of people!"

The worst part, however, is that most Orthodox Jews do not work and instead let themselves be supported by the state of Israel. That just brings me to my knees. In my opinion, there isn't any real difference between Orthodox Jews and Muslim fundamentalists. They're equally fanatical and equally stubborn and one can't talk with either of them. Together they're going to pull it off, destroying this country.

In the summer of 1997, a bombing took place in *Mahane Yehuda*, the Jewish Market in Jerusalem. I had been on the spot where the explosion happened just an hour before. I buy chicken parts there for my cats twice a week. Two men blew themselves up on the corner of a small alley and fifteen people died. Everything in the area was destroyed. The fellow I visit for chicken was miraculously unharmed. I was there at 12 pm and needed to pick up more things, but it became too crowded for me on that day and so I decided to go home. Whenever I get caught in large gatherings of people, I leave, always. I arrived home at 1pm and heard the news on the radio. I then switched on the television and saw the man I had just been standing across from in a complete state of shock, running through the street. Two days later, I returned to the market and to him. Not a word was uttered between us about it, but it appeared that he smiled at me for the first time since we've known each other. One doesn't really talk about these things. What can you really offer besides platitudes? There's just nothing you can say.

In this country, people learn to live with these things. I remember well what I felt in the spring of 1996, when inside of one week two buses exploded, one after the other. Each time it was the #18 bus, which runs near my home, happening at 7am while I was in bed. When I heard the explosion I knew immediately–that's not a jet fighter breaking the sound barrier. Forty people were killed. The feeling is beyond description. I thought to myself, "Here you are, lying comfortably in your bed, and a few meters from here, innocent young people have just been blown apart."

They say the suicide bombers are promised seventy-two virgins in paradise as their reward–what a fine thing. But all religions have their hands nicely soiled with blood. Nationalism, chauvinism, and religion cooked up together are the best ingredients for war and terror. It always works. Religious people, regardless which ones, distinguish themselves chiefly through a sense of being constantly offended. They're always hurt and feeling themselves under attack. As a result, there is a lack of respect for others' religions, as they believe theirs is the only correct one. In Islam, for example, there is so much talk about the horrible fate that awaits the infidels and unbelievers. And we ourselves call non-Jews, quite disparagingly, "the uncut, the uncircumcised." Each is ready to slit the other's throat for his own God and a place in paradise. I am not religious, but I do believe one should give consideration to the feelings of those who are. The religious, however, should also give some consideration to my feelings, but this seems to be impossible for them. I'm not speaking only about Islam here, but also about the Orthodox Jews who want to force their way of life upon me. One person may believe in superstitions about black cats, another believes in something else...they can believe in whatever they want, but they should leave me alone.

When Arabs truly hate someone, it can become deadly, but the same can also be true when they like you. They practically kill you with their kindness. To be invited over to an Arab household for dinner—oh, may God protect you from this! Just to visit and have merely one little drink or a little snack together is completely and utterly impossible. That would be an insult. When you go, you must go fully prepared. Arab hospitality means, among other things, eating until you explode. With Bedouins, it's really bad. Just as you arrive, a sheep is taken out back around the corner and for a second you lose your appetite. You hear it going "bah bah!" in the background and realize—that's dinner. Not quite everyone likes such a sound, you know. The invitation is an honor and an occasion, but you must know just how to behave and what to say. The greetings begin with *Ahlan wa-Sahlan* and "How are your children and the rest of the family?" And again *Ahlan* and once more *Sahlan*, the whole thing top to bottom again, side to side, forwards and backwards. Words run thin when everyone doesn't really share the same tongue and you can wind up nodding or shaking the head a good deal. You can't talk about the weather either because it's always the same here: the sun shines and it's hot. Among Bedouins, eating is done with the right hand. It's important to shape the rice just right, and to know how much to eat. Eat too much, and you will lose respect. Eat too little and your host will be insulted. After a third cup of coffee, you should turn the cup over as a sign you don't wish to have another. To turn it over after the second cup would be improper, upsetting your host who'll think you didn't like the coffee. It's all very ceremonious, but truly comfortable it is not.

Yet it's still endurable with Bedouins, sitting quite romantically on the floor, resting on heaps of pillows, clouds of smoke rising all around. It conjures up images of "Lawrence of Arabia." In contrast, with the well-to-do Arabs, one sits in large tacky upholstered chairs staring directly across at each other. The women peek out from the kitchen and likewise the rest of the relatives. I assume that when the guest finally leaves, they're just as relieved as the he is—only their honor prevents them from admitting it. It's all about honor among the Arabs. The Israelis to this day have not grasped this, I think. For example, when an Arab man goes with his family down the street, you cannot just stop him, pat him down for weapons, and make him hold his hands up in the air—all right in front of his children's eyes. That just won't work, this sort of treatment, and he can never forgive someone for it. An Arab policeman could do this, but we may not.

CHAPTER EIGHT

Although I do not believe that it will bring peace, I am one hundred percent in favor of finally giving back the West Bank. Israel has since become strong enough to allow it. Besides, what difference do borders really make these days when in the event of war missiles can simply be fired across them? We witnessed this during the Gulf War, which I survived inside my sealed up apartment. We were helpless back then as Iraqi missiles made with German know-how were landing on Tel Aviv. And the Palestinian population danced on the rooftops.

Perhaps there are people or societies that can afford to lose a war. Germany, for example, lost the war and is better off than ever before. The Arabs have lost every war but always come out the winners. We, in contrast, cannot afford it, not even to lose a single war. The war that we lose against the Arabs would most certainly be our last, since the Arabs are not only bad losers, they're also bad winners. There wouldn't be a single stone left standing in Israel. And in New York, they would hold a moment of silence, lay some wreaths, and say "Such a pity for this courageous little nation."

The right-wing Israelis maintain that returning the West Bank would not appease the Arabs, that they'll simply always want more. All right, maybe it is true that they'll still want more, but everyone can desire more. I would like to have a Rolls Royce too, but that doesn't mean I'll get one. Granted, they want Ramle, they want Lod, also Haifa, and finally Tel Aviv. You cannnot take action against their thoughts just because they want these things. In Germany there are refugees from Silesia[1] who want to have Silesia back. And why shouldn't they? I wish for Pomerania[2] to become part of Germany again, and to have Kolberg[3] back. Why shouldn't I? It is permissible to want these things, but it will never come to pass. Germany started the war, and in the end, Greater Germany became a smaller country. That's how it is. Does anyone seriously think of returning that lost territory to the Germans?

I am not a chauvinist and, as I say, I would rather give back the West Bank today than tomorrow. But it annoys me when I read in German papers: "The Israelis occupied the West Bank." I ask myself then, what exactly is this supposed to mean? Do they mean that we got up one morning and strolled into the West Bank to occupy it, just like that? The Arabs started The Six-Day War, not us. I witnessed it. Why did Hussein have to lead a war against us? In 1948 the Jordanians had already annexed the West Bank and East Jerusalem. If in 1967 he had stayed put in Amman, then all of that would still belong to him today.

Or the Golan Heights: How did the Golan Heights fall to Israel? The world seems to believe that the Israelis decided one day, "Today we conquer the Golan Heights!" Poor Syrians! As if for fifty years they hadn't been stirring up trouble from atop the mountain shooting at anything down below that moved. The youngsters in the kibbutzim slept in bomb shelters for years. When the Syrians had control of the Golan Heights, did they leave us alone? It wasn't enough for them. Did they want Haifa too perhaps? The Syrians were up there in the hilltops, we were down below, and it bothered them that we tended to our fields in the valley, so every now and then they shot at Israeli fisherman on Lake Genezareth. The UN report would say: "An unidentified person was killed." They didn't give any details, as usual. They pretended not to know the victim was an Israeli, nor who had done the shooting. Maybe it was the Chinese! When we shot back, however, that was made very clear in UN reports, always speaking of an "Israeli overreaction." Once, just before the American singer and activist Joan Baez was to perform in Caesarea, the Arabs had been shooting across the border. Baez said to the audience that she was alarmed, but appealed to the Israelis, "Please no retaliation!" I asked myself then, why does she make appeals to us? Why doesn't she implore *them,* those who did the shooting in the first place, "Please, don't shoot!"

My friend Carol, an American Jewish girl who was married to an Egyptian man, was doing research in Israel and her husband came to visit her. She was of the opinion that the Golan Heights should be returned. So I said to her, "Go and show your husband the Golan Heights, and ask him, an Arab, if we should hand it back. He will think it's a crazy idea, I guarantee it." She didn't take him there, but anyone who has seen the area, even ultra-leftists, hold the opinion afterward that the Golan Heights should not be returned under any circumstances. Not for the sake of the infra-structure we built there, but solely for strategic reasons. Giving it back wouldn't help anyway. The Golan Heights indeed belonged to the Syrians for years. And was there any peace then?

I never dreamt of a Greater Israel, and slowly the ma-jority of Israelis are coming to their senses, realizing it was a major mistake not to have listened to Ben Gurion and Moshe Dayan, when after the Six-Day War they said, "Re-turn everything immediately." Even Prime Minister Levy Eshkol supported a return of the territories. And when asked what would happen then, he replied in Yiddish, "A kleinere Medine, a shenere Medine"—A smaller country, a more beautiful country.

Today we know that it's true, and that we could have spared ourselves a lot of trouble. Who needs these territo-ries anyway? We've already got enough to do taking care of ourselves without having to manage an additional three million Arabs! We should leave them alone and let them govern themselves. If one wants to know how it is when Arabs govern themselves, just look at Lebanon. Everyone would rather be kept in line by their own police, includ-ing the Palestinians. Why should we be the ones to do it? And why should we be supervising their children's educa-tion? Previously four out of five Arab infants died, today all five survive thanks to Israeli public health services. We've brought them a bit of modern civilization. Now the time has come for them to take care of these things for them-selves and for us to take care of our own problems. There is a reason why I never got in the habit of visiting Bethlehem, the Old City, or elsewhere in the West Bank since 1967, even though it's all just around the corner from me and visible from my terrace. I would love to go to Bethlehem in good conscience and eat hummus and lamb, not as an occupier, but as a visitor.

Kurt Tucholsky once said that there can be men without legs and men without arms, but never men without flags! If we hadn't been so foolish, we would have recognized this earlier. The problem isn't that we conquered their land, but something much worse: we took away their honor. Something like this does not go unpunished. One can take a great deal away from a people, but never their honor. Maybe we failed to see that because we were only aware of our own past oppression. As it says in the Bible, "The worst kind of slave-holder is a former slave."

Nevertheless, we came to this country with many ideals. We had seen the mistakes of the other older countries, among democracies and dictatorships alike, and believed we could construct something completely new. And today I see we have managed to make all the same mistakes that they did. We too have become a country like all other countries; one part of the population works, another sits around doing nothing, and another governs. Bureaucrats are like amoebas, they always multiply; one office soon becomes two. They make a great deal of fuss, taking lots of surveys and sending out tons of letters, which up until recently, were stapled closed so you'd poke your finger opening them. At least we got rid of those. But the bureaucrats

are busy regulating this and that, how large an imported car may be, or how small, and how many people should sit inside. They hassle the entire population. In my view the state should look after public transport, waste disposal, the health system, the police, and that's it. Their guiding motto should be, "Be nice to your people, since they're the ones who pay the taxes." The state should leave people alone who basically just want to take a vacation or maybe buy a bigger refrigerator. Happy are a people who do not know the name of their Prime Minister. Such a thing does exist. The majority of Swiss do not know the name of their Prime Minister, but they do know the name of their town mayor and their district nurse. They also know what time their trains and buses leave. We know the names of all our ministers, but not when the trains and buses leave.

Society needs politicians just like it needs garbage collection. But politicians shouldn't be allowed to stay too long in office and must be tossed out every few years. On the kibbutz, I worked on a citrus plantation for a time. We didn't have a tap for drinking water so one of the workers suggested, "Let me fetch the water and you take over my work." We agreed and so he left, but it took quite some time before he made it back with the water, strolling the whole way. The next day he shows up later than the rest of us, knowing we wouldn't need the water until after having worked a while. Now he has a pencil in hand to count all the rows we'd tilled so we didn't have to do it ourselves. Eventually he started collecting up the tools at the end of the day, accounting for them and storing them away. Soon we stopped seeing him at all while we worked and then one day, he drove into the city with a briefcase in his hand to begin organizing something. Now, I suspect he's in the Knesset, maybe bringing drinking water to its members and counting the rows. There may be no tools there for him to collect at the day's end, but he's considered a worthy member of society.

All the self-appointed tree and tool counters and water carriers of the world sit in parliaments everywhere. Nothing against them, but after a certain period of time they should go back to work again so they don't forget what that is. This doesn't happen though, and the whole world winds up being controlled by busy-body bureaucrats who just keep track of everything all the time.

I've often thought that perhaps politicians around the world should change places with one another on a constantly rotating basis. Some years back when Yitzhak Shamir[4] was still Prime Minister, I wished he and German Chancellor Kohl could have changed places. Kohl, who was for a Palestinian state, would have been good for us while Shamir, in return, would have opposed German reunification. In 1997 Netanyahu could have been President of the United States and King Hussein might have governed Israel for a few years. Hussein could've brought a little more zest into affairs here and seen to it that state guests were properly received. Nobody receives VIPs at the airport like Hussein, with his military band and Bedouin bagpipers. Perhaps he also might have generated some understanding for the Jewish people, or maybe not, but either way

Israel would've been a kingdom. In earlier times, all the royal houses and dynasties mixed; the King of Greece was a Prussian, and the King of England, the German Kaiser, and Czar Nicholas, were cousins. And if that didn't work out well it was probably because there's always fighting going on inside families. But today a rotating system for politicians might be just the thing we need for a lasting peace.

In the 1960's Israelis started to travel abroad. Up until that time anyone who traveled to Europe was still a sensation. Back then, all the friends would be invited over and they would sit around the living room gawking at the recently-returned as if he'd come back from the moon. He'd have to tell all about what the people did and didn't do, how they dressed, the latest gossip, and of course, what was still there.

I had a friend who went to the 1958 World Exhibition in Brussels, and then on to Nuremberg where his family had owned a factory before the war. When he returned, his friends in Jerusalem wanted to know everything; what was left of the factory, what had the Germans said to him, and how his first contact with them had been. We were completely isolated and knew absolutely nothing about the rest of the world. There was no television in Israel, not until 1967. Golda Meir wouldn't allow it.

The first time I went back to Germany was in 1966, and I went with very mixed feelings. For thirty years I had felt a great longing, not for Germany necessarily, but for the European climate and atmosphere. I wanted to smell the air after it rains, I wanted just a little sunshine and regular temperatures—cool in the morning, warm in the afternoon, evenings cool again. Not so extreme like it is here.

My flight stopped first in Italy. In my opinion, Southern Italy is still the Middle East. In Israel they say that the only Arab country which hasn't declared war on Israel is Sicily.

As we flew on to Munich, I wondered how I would feel in the *hauptstadt der bewegung*, "the capital of the (Nazi) movement." I got off the plane and felt… nothing. I wasn't agitated or anxious, I wasn't pleased, but neither was I sad. Indeed in Berlin I felt somehow at home, yet not in a sentimental way. Entering a subway station, that distinctive smell of Berlin's *U-Bahn* hit me going down the stairs. Then something happened: As I looked into the faces of pensioners on the subway, I started asking myself, what did they do during the Third Reich? I knew not every single German had been a Nazi, but I couldn't avoid it.

What really got on my nerves in Germany, however, wasn't the old or the new Nazis, not even the casual anti-Semitic expressions, but the German philo-Semites. It bothers me to this day. The people are absolutely beside themselves when they hear you come from Israel; "Oh my God!" And then it starts: the Jews that they knew, and still more Jews they had known, and their Jewish neighbors… and finally: "We had no clue!" Sooner or later comes this sentence. It's unavoidable evidently. I even believe them when I hear it, but feel they don't have to say it. I don't really want to hear how they didn't know what was happening. They could at least have the tact not to say this to me. But it rumbles inside of them, deep inside, and will continue doing so for a long time to come. Then there's the other classic sentence that really gets to me: "We suffered too." What do they mean, "We suffered too"? Have they forgotten why? They brought it on themselves! Now they complain. They should go have a look at the old newsreels and remember rallying for their *führer* when they're feeling like that.

Not for a moment in my life did I ever feel the desire to move back to Germany. They threw me out and that was their loss, not mine. Anti-Semitism is the anti-Semite's problem, not the Jews'. Of course we have our troubles with it, as anti-Semitism is worse than plain antipathy. Antipathies are normal. The Bavarians, for example, hate the Prussians, yet that isn't lethal. Anti-Semitism, in contrast, can be lethal. There's a story of how a Jew and an anti-Semite meet. The anti-Semite says, "I have one eye made out of glass and if you can tell which one it is, I will let you live." The Jew replies, "The left eye is glass." The anti-Semite asks, "How could you tell?" The Jew replies, "It looks so human." Only those who are stuck in the past are still classic anti-Semites. Today, it's all too easy for people to live out their anti-Semitic feelings simply by being anti-Israel.

Israelis, meanwhile, have become a people like all others and differ only in small ways. Before, when *goyim* did something that was uncouth to Jews, there was always a quick exchange of glances and a murmer of "G.N.," and that said it all. G.N. is short for *Goyim Naches*. The term is difficult to explain, but it implies a proletarian satisfaction, sort of lower class. When someone hangs up rice paper lanterns at night from their balcony and puts on an *italienische nacht*[1] then you have G.N. When people sit around drinking beer, grilling, and whenever possible, singing harmonica songs, that's G.N. *Goyim Naches* is also *eisbein*, braised ham hock covered in crispy fat, with sauerkraut. *Eisbein* is a typically German culinary atrocity, not so much because it isn't kosher, but because it's something a Jew simply wouldn't eat. Octoberfest is without a doubt G.N., and Father's Day trips are first class G.N. Boxing and mountain hikes, likewise. The Rosenblums, a family for whom my mother worked several years, were friends with the manager of the King David Hotel, a non-Jew from Switzerland. Once he stopped by to visit and while slightly tipsy, smacked the glass surface of the table with his cane,

Jerusalem 1975

just fooling around. That's when Mrs. Rosenblum leaned over and whispered to my mother: "G.N!"

So now we have our own *Goyim Naches*. What the Moroccans in Israel do, for example, is definitely G.N.; namely outdoor picnics. It's really horrific. They take everything along except the kitchen sink. There's the grill, the radio, even the television, which they hook up to the car. And the wife, instead of washing the dishes at home in comfort, stands in Lake Genezareth up to her knees in water and washes up there. The man sits in his folding chair, watching TV and smoking his cigar. The kids holler and the mosquitoes bite, the pita bread gets filled with charred meat and a little bit of sand, and you do this and you do that, and in the evening everyone drives home dead tired and collapses. With luck, there's even a little auto accident on the way home too. In short: *Goyim Naches!*

For several years now, I've had a German passport again, not for sentimental reasons but because it's very practical for traveling. You hold it up and you pass on through. The Israeli passport on the other hand, is handled by border and security officials the world over as if it might just explode. You always have to step out from the line. Once when I arrived in Sweden and showed my Israeli passport, the official asked after a suspicious long hard look at it, "Tourist?" I said, "No. Terrorist." That broke the ice.

Sometimes I ponder living in Berlin for a few months, but not for longer, mostly when the Jewish nationalists here get too much on my nerves. This country has changed into something else, and I must say, it has not become what we once dreamt of. We were prepared for anything, but not for

Next to a portrait of his father, Berlin 1970's

a kosher state. That was never our intention! We wanted to form a socialist state and not a theocracy.

Ultimately, we have to blame Ben Gurion for this. He was a socialist himself, but like all those who came from Eastern Europe back then, had a huge respect for anyone who grew a long beard and let himself be addressed as *"Rebbe."* The socialists said, "You wish to have a kosher state?—So you shall have it, but in return, don't mix in the affairs of foreign policy." The secularists underestimated the power of the religious parties. Shimon Peres himself was so sentimental and preferred going with the religious and observant ones rather than with the leftists. Nevertheless, he didn't benefit from it as he lost the election anyway. He would read one book every sinlge night, he said. One doesn't elect such a man.

Up to now, Yitzhak Rabin has been the one and only Prime Minister who wasn't beholden to the religious groups, and that cost him his life! They cursed him, conducted a smear campaign, and they stirred up so much hatred until one of these nuts shot him. Afterwards people were shocked and a little ashamed and the rabbis were quiet for two weeks. Then the murder of Yitzhak Rabin became an act of God for the religious and the murderer was just a misguided boy.

I worry about the future of Israel. The observant flock to this country in droves to treat their inferiority complexes. We've become the insane asylum for the world's Jewry. The religious fanaticism, the blindness and stubbornness here is appalling. When a faith degenerates into superstition, things become dangerous. Here one is constantly preoccupied with religion, concerned with how best to be observant. Now they've even invented a telephone that can be answered without breaking the rules of Shabbat. And people make a living from this!

It's like how Yankel says to Moishe, "One hears so much about this Albert Einstein and his theory of relativity these days. Can you explain it to me?" So Moishe says, "It's like this: When you stick your nose up my behind then I have a nose in the ass and you have a nose in the ass. It's all

With a friend in Jerusalem

relative though." Yankel then wonders to himself and says, "And Einstein makes a living with that?"

It's the same among the religious and observant types here. They study *Gemara* and *Talmud* and sit around the whole day debating the difference between selling oxen for work or for slaughter. Young men hang out in the *yeshivas* who aren't employed and don't do anything, and receive social support for it. Later they go out into to the world and give out *Kashrut* stamps. That's how they live. An entire population is developing into parasites and a kind of collective religious insanity is supported. That's not my country. That is not the sort of thing we once dreamed of creating.

With cat "Mottek" on his terrace in Jerusalem

When I travel to Germany these days, I am often asked, "What is your *heimat* (homeland) actually?" I don't know how to respond to the question. Who is still living in the same place where he was born these days? *Heimat* is an idealization, it's something one longs to return to. When speaking of *heimat* people often mean the loss of youth in some way. *Heimat* for me is the place where I get annoyed about government officials and where my bed is, where I can lay my head down. I believe I could get along most anywhere, but I would always come back to Israel.

Today I am a gentleman of leisure, very busy with doing nothing, and for that one needs lots of time and talent.

My friends probably appreciate my absence of of ambition. I don't represent any threat to them. People like it when there's someone around who's not ambitious, who doesn't desire a bigger car, a larger apartment, who is content with what he has. I think people like me because I'm harmless, I don't bother them, and I don't take anything away from them. I don't want to have their jobs, and I don't want to have their wives. For God's sake, no.

I live with a neurotic cat and that's all I need. Mottek is completely insane. She is over 25 years old and doesn't hear so well anymore. She wakes me up around six in the morning with her meowing, and then when I finally do get up, she just puts one paw over the eyes and goes back to sleep. What do I need a wife for when I have this cat? Her meowing drives me crazy. I've chased after her with a broom at 3am. Life with Mottek fulfills me completely.

Every Saturday is open house at my place. The only thing I offer is coffee. Whosoever wants to have cake or pastries must bring them along. I am considered to be the best joke-teller in town, and I hope I live up to that reputation. Sometimes I perform in clubs or retirement homes, usually beginning my routine with something our Polish foreman said at a kibbutz assembly in 1939. He believed he was speaking formal high German, but what came out was in absolutely perfect Yiddish: "Ich will heut sprechen zu eich in die Sprache vun Gethe und Schilla!" ("Today I'd like to speak to you in the language of Goethe and Schiller!")

I was never bored a single day of my life; each day was interesting. There was always something happening, something going on here. This country pulls crazy folks in like a magnet. If they were to put a roof over it, it would be a closed mental institution. Everybody here is searching for themselves. I don't know why everyone has to go searching for their identity. For me, they told me my name and that was all I needed.

Of course there are people who always think of the future, who prepare for it, like a squirrel getting ready for the winter when it's still summer. I have never prepared for winter, and now winter is here, but I am not cold. In Israel, everyone lives close to God and everybody can speak to him directly. Somebody should ask him why he had to create the world in just six days. What was the big hurry? From the looks of things here sometimes, it would have been better if he'd taken a bit more time with it!

* * *

Ahlan wa-Sahlan:	Arabic welcoming greeting
Baruch ha-Shem:	Praise unto God
challah:	Egg rich yeast leavened bread usually braided or twisted and eaten traditionally on Shabbat and holidays
chalutzim:	Pioneers, settlers
chaver:	Comrade, kibbutz member
chedar mishpachah:	Room for a married couple/family on the kibbutz
Eretz Yisrael:	The biblical land of Israel
Etzel:	Abbreviation for *Irgun Zvai Leumi,* "National Military Organization," a nationalistic military underground group founded in 1937 out of the ranks of Jabotinsky revisionists and led by Menachem Begin from 1943 on
gabbai:	A collector mostly for a synagogue council, or a secretary
Ghaffir:	Guard, auxiliary policeman
gefilte fish:	Traditional Ashkenazi dish made of minced carp and other fish

Gemara:	Rabbinical commentaries and analysis on the Mishnah
Glubb Pasha:	Nickname of John Bagot, British officer, commander of the Arab Legion, military advisor to King Hussein until 1957
Goyim Naches:	Literally "pleasures of non-Jews"; things Jews aren't supposed to do
hachsharah:	Job training in preparation for immigration to Palestine
Haganah:	"Protection," an underground Jewish military organization, founded 1920, forerunner to the Israeli army
High Commissioner:	Head of British administration in during the mandate period
Jewish Agency for Palestine:	Organ of the Zionist world organization, essentially the Jewish government in Palestine before statehood
Jewish Settlement Police:	Jewish auxiliary police set up by the British primarily in the service of guarding settlements
Jugend-Alijah:	Organization for Jewish youths moving to Palestine, founded 1933 in Berlin
Kashrut:	Catalog of rules and rituals in Judaism regarding purity and cleanliness in diet and keeping a household kosher
Mishnah:	Canonical collection of Jewish oral law
mishpacha:	Hebrew for family; Yiddish: mischpoche

Palmach:	Elite unit of the Jewish self-defense group *Haganah*, founded in 1941
rebbe:	Charismatic figure, can be though mustn't necessarily be a trained rabbi
sabras:	Literally a prickly-pear cactus fruit, but the term is also applied to native-born Israelis
Shabbes:	Yiddish for Shabbat, Sabbath
shammes:	Synagogue caretaker
shofar:	Horn of a ram, blown at the start of the Jewish New Year and on Yom Kippur
tallis, tallit:	Prayer shawl made from wool
Talmud:	Authoritative body of Jewish tradition comprised of the *Mishnah* and *Gemara*
yekke:	Name applied to German Jews typically preoccupied with order and rules
yeshiva:	Religious school for study often in preparation for becoming a rabbi

ENDNOTES

CHAPTER ONE

1. Alexander Granach was born in Galicia, today part of southeastern Poland but then part of the Austro-Hungarian Empire.

2. Anarcho-syndicalism – Revolutionary trade unionist movement that embraced Marxist theory of class struggle culminating in collective ownership of goods and production but rejected the Marxist concept of government by proletarian dictatorship.

3. Henrik Ibsen – Norwegian dramatist known for his realistic portrayals of social problems. Aimed to make the European middle class confront themselves and the faulty aspects of their value system.

4. One of Berlin's most famous boulevards, rife with cafés, restaurants, and shopping.

5. Arnolt Bronnen – Dramatist, narrative writer, essayist. Most performed dramatist of the Weimar Republic. Switched many times between extreme left and right positions. Worked with Brecht in from 1922-26. Member of Nazi party in the 1930s. Joined Austrian Resistance in '43. Moved to GDR in 1955.

6. Hermine Koerner – Theater actress. From 1919-25 manager and artistic director for Munich's Schauspielhaus, Lustspieltheater, and Kuenstlertheater.

7. KaDeWe – Kaufhaus des Westens, translates as "Shopping Hall of the West," a massive Berlin mall offering all types of wares and still popular today.

8. Kurt Tucholsky – Poet, essayist, critic, satirist, was one of the most widely read authors during the Weimar Republic. He was among the first to be stripped of citizenship as the Nazis seized power.

9. Prussian Breslau and Posen are now Wroclaw and Posen, Poland.

10. USPD – Independent Social Democratic Party of Germany (Unabhaengige Sozialdemokratische Partei Deutschlands)

11. SPD – German Social Democratic Party (Sozialdemokratische Partei Deutschlands)

12. Traven wrote about issues of social justice, cruelty, and greed while employing a taut suspenseful style. His early works dealt with tramps either looking for work or having found it temporarily, and in this process being caught in a worldwide exploitative system.

13. *Mutual Aid: A Factor of Evolution* by the Russian social reformer and philosopher Prince Pyotr Kropotkin who theorized that cooperation and not competition was the basis of evolutionary survival.

14. Indian books (Indianerbuecher) were and continue to be immensely popular in Germany. The most beloved author in this genre was Karl May, through whom most Germans receive an indelible impression of what the American Wild West was like. In contrast to American nostalgia for the Wild West, these stories were told from the Native Americans' point of view, not that of the cowboys'. Interestingly, as vivid as the depiction of the landscape and people were, May had never been to America. He wrote strictly from imagination, completing his most famous works while in jail.

15. Bronislaw Hubermann – Polish violin virtuoso. Performed all over the world and formed the Palestine Symphony Orchestra in 1935, made up almost exclusively of Jewish refugees.

16. Yehudi Menuhin – American violin virtuoso who had impressed audiences since the age of seven. At age thirteen he inspired Einstein to declare at a Berlin concert, "Now I know there is a God in Heaven!" His recordings are widely available today. Died in Berlin in 1999.

17. Walter Rathenau served five months as Germany's foreign minister in 1922 until assassinated by two right wing army officials.

18. Otto Lilienthal – inventor and aeronautical pioneer. The Wright Brothers considered him their hero and the most important figure of the 19th century. Studied bird flight, conducting pre-Wright experiments and wrote *Birdflight as the Basis of Aviation*. Lilienthal was indeed Jewish.

19. Alexander Kerensky later became Russia's Minister of War. Immigrates 1940 to U.S. Joined staff of the Hoover Institution on War Revolution and Peace at Stanford University.

20. Fun-to-read educational books for children

21. German has two forms for addressing the 2nd person "you"; they are the formal and respectful "Sie" and the informal "du". One addresses strangers, business partners, or anyone else aside from family and friends almost exclusively with the "Sie" form. Though it would still be highly irregular to use "du" in the classroom today, the fact that it occurred in Granach's grade school in the 1920s is extraordinary and underscores its alternative character.

22. Sergi Eisenstein's 1925 film about the uprising on the Battleship Potemkin conceived as class conscious revolutionary propaganda. Kids having just seen the action-filled movie may have enjoyed recreating its scenes on the playground.

23. Qualification exam for university acceptance similar to American S.A.T.s.

24. Erwin Piscator – modernist theater director who saw theater as a conscious and theorized response to needs of a particular historical movement. Taught acting to Marlon Brando and James Dean during exile in the U.S.; Klabund – pseudonym of Alfred Henschke, expressionist poet, writer, and dramatist; Heinrich George – actor, film star, and director of the Schiller Theater in Berlin. Collaborated with Nazis appearing in the anti-Semitic film *Jud Suess* (1940); Erich Muehsam – writer, poet, dramatist, and anarchist. Took part in the uprising of Bavaria in 1919. Among the 4000 arrested on night the Reichstag was set on fire in 1933 just one day before his intended flee to Switzerland. Tortured and killed by the Nazis.

25. Avus were something of a predecessor to the autobahns.

26. Shylock – Central character of Shakespeare's *The Merchant of*

Venice who, depending on the actor's portrayal and the director's vision, can come across in a horribly anti-Semitic way or as a figure with whom the audience may sympathize. The disparate portrayals of Shylock and the question of Shakespeare's original intent have been a topic of some debate for a very long time.

27. Chenio Vinaver was also a musicologist and conductor specializing in Chassidic choral music. Immigrated to New York City in 1938, and later to Israel.

28. Joachim Prinz – prominent rabbi in Berlin and a vehement proponent of the Zionist cause. Writes book *Wir Juden* ("We Jews") in 1934 making clear his stance against assimilation and mixed marriages. Perceived the National Socialist revolution in Germany would mean Germany for the Germans and "Jews for Jewery" and result in a hastening of emigration to Palestine. Foreign Jewish observers at the time saw Prinz as Zionism's most strident advocate.

29. Mascha Kaleko – heralded as a young talent in the tradition of Tucholsky, she published two highly successful volumes celebrating and satirizing life in the late Weimar Republic before being forced into exile. Kaleko was originally from Galicia.

30. Fritzi Massary – major star of operettas (romantic comic opera that includes song and dance) forced to flee Germany in 1933. Retired 1938 in Beverly Hills, California.

31. The Volksbuehne was designed by Oskar Kaufman, a master architect who designed numerous theaters in Berlin and Vienna. Immigrated to Palestine in 1933 and built the famous Hebrew theater Habima (1937) in Tel Aviv.

32. Elisabeth Bergner – actress, born in Galicia. Oscar nomination for Best Actress in 1935 for her performance as Gemma Jones in *Escape Me Never*.

33. Ernst Busch – actor, singer, socialist, performed in many Brecht pieces. Interned in France during the war. Released to Germans and sentenced to death by the Nazis but saved when actor and Nazi collaborator Gustaf Gruendgens intervened on his behalf.

34. Victor Barnowsky – directed at several theaters in Berlin, known for his sound grasp of Expressionist theatrical style.

35. Leopold Jessner – Innovative director associated with German Expressionist Theater. Both Jewish and a socialist he went into exile in 1933. Directed at the Habimah Theater in Tel Aviv in 1936 before coming to the US in '37 and settling in Los Angeles.

36. Claire Waldoff – a leading star of the Berlin cabaret scene up until the Nazi clampdown on artists; Friedrich Wolf - prominent doctor and writer known especially for his anti-fascist activism; Erich Kaestner – children's book author, lyricist, and satirist whose books were burned and banned by the Nazis; Erich Muehsam - poet and anarchist, died in Oranienburg concentration camp.

37. Veit Harlan – actor, starred in Nazi film adaptation of *Jud Suess*; Renee Stobrawa – German film actress; Fritz Genschow – actor, producer, director, appears in 1943 German film *Titanic*.

38. Emil Jennings – actor, played opposite Marlene Dietrich as the professor in *The Blue Angel*; Werner Kraus – actor, starred in *The Cabinet of Dr. Caligari*.

39. Burschenschaftlers were members of a quasi-student fraternity engaged in dueling and had characteristics of the Hitler Youth. Initiation rites included cutting a slit on the faces of members to be.

CHAPTER TWO

1. Joseph Schmidt – gifted operatic tenor and a beloved figure in German opera and cinema. Forced to flee Germany at the zenith of his career (including an appearance at Carnegie Hall) he came to Switzerland where he was forced to live and work in a refugee camp. Those who resisted were threatened with deportation to the Nazis.

2. Konrad Wolf – feature film director in the GDR. The Konrad Wolf Film Academy Babelsberg is located today in Potsdam.

3. Carola Neher – actress starred in G.W. Pabst's film version of The Three Penny Opera; disappeared in Russian prison camps.

CHAPTER TWO CONTINUED

4. Lion Feuchtwanger – German-Jewish writer best known for his novel *Jew Suss*. Among first to have citizenship revoked by the Nazis, he fled Europe during the war coming to Los Angeles and from there helped Bertoldt Brecht to escape.

5. Molotov – Soviet Premier from 1930-41 and first engaged as foreign minister '39-49.

6. Alfred Polgar – Viennese Jewish writer, critic, and translator. Fled the Nazis in 1933. Employed by MGM Studios.

7. Alfred Doeblin – wrote the famous epic *Alexanderplatz* which characterized Berlin during the Weimar years. Later adapted into an epic 15 hour film by Rainer Werner Fassbinder.

CHAPTER FOUR

1. Rosa Luxemburg and Karl Liebknecht founded the Sparticist League, a left-wing faction of the Social Democratic Party comprised of revolutionary German socialists. In 1919 they reorganized as the Communist Party of Germany and staged an uprising, centered in Berlin, which was put down by government troops who arrested and murdered Luxemburg and Liebknecht.

2. As Germany's Foreign Minister, Rathenau was assassinated by nationalists who opposed his policy of attempting to pay reparations to the Allies after WWI.

3. Haurani – an Arab people from the Hauran mountain region of Syria. Many came to Palestine for work.

4. Yekke – Yiddish term derived from the word "jacket" that came to be applied to German Jews typically preoccupied with order and punctuality. Originates from a cultural difference between Western European Jews who wore shorter jackets and Eastern Jews who wore traditional longer coats.

5. The "Her" part of *Herführer* could be a play on *Herr*, meaning "Mr." combined with *führer* or "leader" becoming "Mr. Over Here Leader."

CHAPTER FIVE

1. The Dead Sea is widely known for its therapeutic benefits.

2. Rudolph Kastner – head of the Zionist Rescue Committee in Budapest during the war who bargained with Nazis such as Adolf Eichmann to save lives. The trial over his alleged collaboration sparked great debate in Israel. He was first found guilty, then the verdict was overturned but not before he was assassinated in 1957.

CHAPTER SEVEN

1. The Straits of Tiran provide the only access to the Israeli port of Eilat at the head of the Gulf of Aqaba. It is a vital shipping corridor for Israel with links to the Red Sea and major sources of petroleum.

2. Pogrom – Russian for "devastation," refers to the organized massacre of Jews. The term was first applied as such in 1881 in czarist Russia, after the assassination of Czar Alexander II by revolutionaries, and for successive Russian pogroms in 1903, 1905, and 1917, which claimed hundreds of thousands of Jewish victims. In Germany the Nazi driven pogrom of 1938 was called "Night of Broken Glass" (German: Kristallnacht).

CHAPTER EIGHT

1. Silesia – Historic region in Central Europe formerly ruled by the Austrian Hapsburgs and annexed by Prussia in 1742. After WWII, almost all of Prussian Silesia revert back to Poland and the German population was expelled. The region today lies mostly within south-western Poland.

2. Pomerania – former province of Prussia on the Baltic Sea. After WWII, the land was partitioned along the Oder river, with the eastern half placed under Polish administration and the western side falling in the Soviet occupation zone (later East Germany).

CHAPTER EIGHT CONTINUED

3. Kolberg – city within the province of Pomerania where former German population was either expelled or murdered by Soviet forces after WWII.

4. Yitzak Shamir – member of the right-wing Likud Party and Prime Minister from 1983 to 1984 as well as from 1986 to 1992.

CHAPTER NINE

1. Italienische nacht (Italian night) in Germany refers to Italian themed soirées that make use of a few stereotypes to inject an air of romanticism and festivity.

* 9 7 8 0 9 8 2 2 2 5 1 1 0 *